BABYLONIAN
MYTH & MAGIC

AN INTRODUCTION

By Joshua Free

With Foreword by Sortilèges

*Originally published as Liber 51 by the
Mardukite Chamberlains*

© 2011, Joshua Free

*Dedicated
to those
who love
all that is
Babylon.*

Babylonian Myth & Magic

ACKNOWLEDGMENTS

Creation & Design by Joshua Free

Foreword by Sortilèges

Interior Art by Jessica Brooks

Front Cover Art by Sarah Banas

www . mardukite . com

TABLE OF CONTENTS

A BRAVE NEW BABYLON
by Sortilèges

Conflict. . . Unrest. . .
  On earth as it is in heaven. . .

At the precipice of a planetary evolution,
  the *world* ends.

It always does.

Global tensions rise to unprecedented heights
with the passing of each day. The *bright future*
once wrought for mankind grows dark for the
race as a whole. To it: arcane philosophy failed;
ageless religion failed; humanistic ideals failed;
and every magick spell and scientific formulae
furthers sealing mortal man in his own self-
made systematic prison, driving the coffin nail
home – a single-track to travel upon furthering
our journey into the *downward spiral* plunging
the world into inevitability. . . *apocalypse*.

And this is my hope for the world, shared from
the depth of my soul and joined in the voices of
many self-honest truth seekers who have seen
for themselves. . . renewal!

The mystics know; the children know; even the *birds* know – the world is *ending*. Of course, this does not imply the blatant physical, material and totalitarian destruction of humans (so let us not employ the same scare tactics of every evangelizing preacher under the sun), it is instead the ending of *a human world*. It has been said in the recorded legends and tablets that this era of *renewal* will give way to the fabled *Golden Age*, a *Brave New World* – a true *new age*. But this is no *new* idea at all, rather it is something predicted by the main tenets of every true spiritual path throughout history, differentiated solely by semantics and appearing as varied as opinions from the *Second Coming of Christ* to the the cosmic collapse of the material universe by some rift in space-time or even *dark matter* and *black holes*.

You can label and interpret, even sugarcoat, what is happening any way you like – the simple fact remains: There is an undeniable feeling shared throughout the collective human consciousness that *something* is about to happen – that something *is* happening – and yet it all seems to endlessly cycle back and forth in some predetermined fragile balance.

So *what* are we to do? While the bungled confusion of the world plagues the mind with anxiety demons and victimization tendencies, the answer couldn't be simpler: *we must provoke the end of the world*, in this case, through a *massive paradigm shift*, meaning the necessary return of the *true spirituality*. By this, I mean the original *stuff*; untainted; undefiled through time by the analytical minds and personal truths of men corrupted into *systems* – fragmented from the whole; never the tween shall meet; *thank you, call back later.*

It may seem like nothing new; but *no*, this time *it is different*.

In the wake of this self-honest planetary need for a *Great Awakening*, and on the cusp of a true *new age*, many 'cults' have risen in recent past, loosely termed 'pagan'. Yet, in all of their once revolutionary efforts marked upon human consciousness, what they have to offer is often really only a 'turn of the wheel', simply providing a different container for the *same content*, proving to us once again that humanity has not evolved since the days of antiquity.

Understand we are not here to tell you what to think, raising 'mardukite literature' to some new authoritarian heights, but we are offering critical information and data correction for your noggin so that you might *self-honestly* think for *yourself*. The emphasis here on *self* is not merely some glorification of individualism or newfangled ego-worship, but an affirmation that if we really want to change the *world*, we had better clean up and change our *self* first. When each human being takes the responsibility to grasp the *self-honest* realizations of who they are and where they come from, what the world is and how it was made, of the stuff dreams and stars are made of, the *universe* and *everything* – when the experience of all these things can be done *honestly* from *self*, then will the race see an end to the current melancholy, heinous non-sense that is happening and has been happening for quite some time – a condition that is actually *anathema* to the survival of the very creatures that keep these things the way they are!

The premises we use to chart a *new world* are simple enough:

- *Every* human being has the potential and responsibility to experience life in *self-honesty*.

- *Every* human being has the right and freedom to demand this of their existence.

- *Every* human being has to embrace *some universal oneness* in order to live in harmony with itself as a race of brethren; with the Earth as a base of homestead; and with the universe as a matrix of existence. Only then can humans experience true *unity with all life, the universe and everything!*

This is our *true* and *destined* existence.

But what has kept man from achieving these ends? Why is it that the shortcomings of humanity throughout history seem to keep repeating recursively? Why has *everything* failed? As with all else, we find that the answer is again quite simple: *because humans are forgetful*.

We forget easily; we are often sad; we suffer; we lose sight. To regain anything meaningful for the present and any hope for the future, we must remember what once was, and fortunately for us, an order of some of the earliest mystics thought of just that – so they created *cuneiform-writing*.

This book, as with the commonly referred to

'cycle' of literature produced by the 'mardukites', is sure to present to you ideas of 'history' and 'magick' in ways you have never seen, or maybe even imagined before. The tradition that it represents does not deal in rudimentary hierarchical *grimoires* or the application of general hermetic principles upon some historical ethno-centric tradition. The 'mardukite' work runs much deeper than even this. It presents *the* system – the archetypal system – that has formed the basis for every mystery tradition to later emerge.

In other words: if you can correctly understand the means and motives of the mysteries and religion of Babylon, you will correctly be able to interpret 'history' and 'magick' as a whole – whatever these words may mean to you. You will become privy to the beauty of the original efforts that have mostly deteriorated with time, probably attaining its lowest evolutionary depths in Christian-controlled medieval Europe – or even in the practices of modern day Jews and Muslims who use religion to shroud political reasons for killing one another. Even more important perhaps, you will become aware of what *really* happened in ancient Babylon, and understand whether or not it really was the *right* way to execute *Divine Order*, and why.

Indeed – the focal point of the modern *mardukite* movement has never been about bringing back the *verbatim* 'Babylonian para-digm' one-to-one, because this would only be the 'turn of the wheel' again, and we've already grown dizzy and tired by such ventures. *This time*, it's all about fixing what went wrong, actually fixing the problem of *systems*, the root of all problems really, at the core. When every individual takes up the *Sword of Truth* against the world, executing the *acid test* of *self-honesty* on reality, then no doubt a *new*, better, *upgraded* aeon will really begin for mankind. This we call: *New Babylon!*

To those who *also* feel called to pursue this with us, we say:

WELCOME HOME!

~ Sortilèges
Spring Equinox, 2011
Bishop-Patesi of Canada
Mardukite Archdiocese of North America

BABYLONIAN
MYTH & MAGIC

AN INTRODUCTION

MARDUKITE

1. ASSYRIOLOGY INTO THE TWENTY-FIRST CENTURY

"When the sculptures and huge, dramatic bas reliefs from Babylon and Nineveh, uncovered by the excavations of Layard and Rawlinson in the mid-19ᵗʰ century, began to arrive in Europe, the people were enthralled but they were also fickle. The greater accessibility of Egypt, and the sheer quantity of the material excavated and exported, pushed Babylon and Assyria into the background, and the civilizations of the Tigris and the Euphrates began to be perceived as colorless and dull, even by esotericists."

~ R.A. Gilbert
Foreword to L.W. King's
Babylonian Magic & Sorcery (2000 Edition)

Mystics of every age have gone forth explaining an almost *quantum* vision of reality and existence, interconnected – *All-as-One.* While this might seem a truly obscure and anomalistic message approach to crossing the threshold of the current 'academic' topic; it is not. Consider for a moment that our *mythic past* is very much rooted in *truth* – one that has simply been conveniently, or forcefully, forgotten among mass awareness. Politics and the general *human condition* have, throughout the ages, taken its toll on the accounts of said *truth*, as we will see quite evidently concerning the history of the geographic region known as *Mesopotamia*.

Humans, being *mortal,* are unaware of one critical aspect of the universe – one that they could not possibly be privy to given their interaction with reality based on limited perceptions and experiences schematized by semantic labeling – is that *truth* is actually *unchanging*. In spite of the best (or worst) efforts in human history, the *truth* has survived to remind us of our origins, to instruct us on where we have to go and perhaps, most importantly, the standards we should live by to get there. Its mere survival is not enough, however, for as the world was once plummeted into a *Dark Age* only to be *reincarnated* as an *Age of Enlightenment*, the *truth* did not appear in public consciousness recognizable as such – in fact, it went the other direction: *underground* and the *vaults* of obscure 'occult' factions.

Unfortunately, the original and intended meaning of the symbolism, used to preserve the integrity of *mysteries*, became as confounded and obscure to these practitioners and 'magicians' as the nature of their own organizations. What's more: they *convinced* themselves that they *did* have true comprehension of it – and so, eventually, the politics of the surface world became no less existent in the underground.

The meaning and innate desire to pursue *truth*, particularly what has been known as the *Secret of the Ages*, is no less obvious in the realm of science and academia then it is in the world of the occultist. Those who have been dubbed 'esotericists' are not the only ones who are interested in these matters, nor are they even the original ones. Only the methodologies and intentions differ. And yet again – all is connected. Without the intellectual and scholarly pursuits by historians and academicians, we might have far fewer clues toward this 'mental image' reconstruction of the past. Where then would the *truth seeker* have to draw his inspiration? From the fanciful recollections of distorted fairy-tales available to the surface world? Certainly, not.

The recovery of the *truth* of mankind's past is paramount to the fate of humanity's future. Thus, it should could by no surprise that the geographic terrain of its origins has been the victim of unyielding war and suffering for thousands of years – further enshrouding those unveiling efforts with a measure of hesitation and doubt painted by political opinions of the modern *Middle East*, and for our purposes, what the academicians have called the *Ancient Near East*. Relative power within the modern world and in human society is a 'fleeting glamour' and wholly representative; yet, if anything on the planet can be said to represent ineffable *true worldly power* by the 'sword' and 'shield' of *truth*, it is from those objects of ancient knowledge that come to us from this place.

For over a century, the pursuit of the *Great Mysteries* of *Babylonia* have been restricted to two main schools: firstly, 19th century academic Assyriology and secondly, the aspects of eso-teric tradition that derived itself from the same. In the first; there are no attempts at philosoph-ical or mystical pragmatism; the entire study field as dry as the sands of the desert inspiring it. In the second; the works of these stoic academicians is used as a basis for revived mystical tradition – often giving little regard for the *specifics* of the *system*, requiring additional facets of knowledge that directly appear nowhere on the fractured clay tablets or vases excavated from the ancient sites.

Fortunately, the 21st century *truth seeker* has a *third* option for their pursuits.

In 2008, a revolutionary organization known as the *mardukites* appeared on the scene, publicly visible – a completely new breed of *next generation* 'Assyriologists' and 'esotericists' alike that would not blindly accept the data given to them by their predecessors – at least not at *face value*. For several years the diversely organized group has sought out the most ancient render-ings and writings found on clay tablets from *Babylonia* and shown the integral link between these and what can be found concerning the remainder of the evolution of human civilization. The methodologies used and the *truth* revealed concerning the identity, natures and progression of this *incredible* subject matter are undeniably superior to what was even available to those who came before us. But, that is what we call *progress* (much needed for this field). More so, we certainly do not deny the contributions of those who provided the modern world these clues their due credit.

The *mardukite* approach to reconstructing the *Babylonian* vision begins with first revealing the incredible misnomer that the field of study has endured for too long. Essentially, the applicable term *Assyriology* is a lie. What's more: it does not actually apply to the current pursuits of *analysis* that are applied to the physical *evidences* brought to light by late 19th and early 20th century archeology. The name questionably applies to the field at all! Even though some of the originating scholars have acknowledged this grave misrepresentation of the science,[1] it has yet gone unchallenged in contemporary academics.

As mentioned, *analysis* and *application* are absent from the originating pursuit, which emphasized mainly only the *recovery* and *accumulation* of the translatable materials, many of which have still yet to be transliterated into English even a century after their discovery. Most of what has been readily available to the *seeker* during the contemporary

---

1 George G. Cameron explains in his foreword to *They Wrote on Clay* (1938) by Edward Chiera that "few there are indeed who know that the name of our science, 'Assyriology' is based on an accident – the fact that the first large group of texts ever discovered were written in Assyrian. Assyrian itself is but *one* dialect." The misapplication concerns the use of the term to denote the study of *any and all* ancient cuneiform using cultures. It can be extended as a blatant disregard for political history given that the Assyrians were actually northwestern *foreigners* to Babylonia.

pre-mardukite era of research and study has been severely fragmented,[2] confounding itself in the relay of content. The variegated cultural influences and often violent history of *Babylonia* has left a confusion of names, titles and images that have required over a century to flush out to any practical ends.

The origins of the name and field of *Assyriology* are derived from the French excavations of *Khorsabad, Nimrud, Nineveh, Sippar* and *Lagash* (*Telloh*) in the 1840's. A true scientific pursuit was ignited when the royal library archives of the Assyrian king *Assur-bani-pal*[3] were discovered, illuminating in cuneiform wedge-writing the clues to a prehistoric legacy formerly thought to be completely

---

2   The earliest attempts are made by "Assriologists" of the late 19th and early 20th century, including: E.A. Budge, Edward Chiera, L.W. King, S.L. Noah Kramer, Franqois Lenormant, R.C. Thompson and L.A. Waddell. These renderings have already received long-standing public attention for those who sought it.

3   Also spelled Ashurbanipal (or Asenappar in the Book of Ezra, *Holy Bible*); heralded the 'last great king' of the Neo-Assyrian empire that occupied Babylon c.7th-8th century B.C. Like the later Hellenistic ruler of Babylon, Alexander the Great, *Assur-bani-pal* sought to collect and preserve all the mysteries of the world in a unifying library.

forgotten and never again salvageable. In the 1880's the Germans uncovered *Babylon*. . .[4]

---

4   Consequently of this period, the vast majority of the tablet transliterations and scholarly commentary (used for the academic approach and in universities) appear solely in either French or German even to this day.

2. A LAND BETWEEN TWO RIVERS

"Here [in Babylon] is real death. Not a column or arch still stands to demonstrate the permanency of human work. Everything has crumbled to dust. The very temple tower, the most imposing of all these ancient constructions, has entirely lost its shape. Where are now its seven stages? We see nothing but a mound of earth – all that remains of the millions of its bricks. Here the ancient mysteries and their tombs have been sleeping quietly for millenniums. In a few months, perhaps in a few days, the ground will be broken by trenches as in a battlefield. And the repose of the poor dead will be disturbed by the frantic search for records and data. . ."

~ Edward Chiera (c. 1930)
From a letter to his wife.

The classical Greeks can be credited with the term: *mesopotamia* – meaning "A land between two rivers." While certainly more literal than poetic, the title accurately describes what was known to the ancients as *Babylonia* – the "Land of the Gates of the Gods" or the "Land of Star-

Gates" secured primarily between two rivers – the *Tigris* and the *Euphrates*. But, before the *seeker* can hope to uncover the more anthropological and mystical concepts of this archaic world, it would be most appropriate to introduce the geography of the region, now known as the *Middle East*, and consequently enshrouded under a political light that thwarts contemporary comprehension. To be successful, you must remove from your sight all of the religious and military drama that has been associated with these places through modern awareness and project yourself into that timeless moment when these things do not exist. From the safety of our text we will walk these wastelands and survey the most critical of the defining natural features.

Commonly compared to the fertile Nile region of Egypt, *Babylonia* is actually also river-delta system – and, like the Nile to the Egyptians, this system of life-giving waters proved to be inseparable from prosperity of the people. The plain was cultivated successfully through the original use of an 'aqueduct-irrigation' system on the planet. The accurate construction and upkeep of these canals were vital to keep *Babylonia* habitable in all seasons. In time, as they were abandoned under foreign control, the dissolution of the aqueduct system resulted in the collapse of *Babylon* as the "throne of the earth" and the lands returned to the indistinct sand they had been built up from.[5]

The exact political boundaries of *Babylonia* are not generally agreed upon – no more today among scholars and nationalists then by those who physically fought for them in periods of antiquity. It is clear that the territory included areas outside the pathway of the two rivers.[6] While not originally called the more familiar names we now know, the lands of *Babylonia* essentially occupy present-day Iraq, in the region bordering on the mountains that separate it (on the east) from Iran, ancient Persia. To the south, the empire once extended to the Persian Gulf where the archetypal city of Eridu was founded. On the western front, Mesopotamia is separated from the Mediterranean and Magan-Egypt by the vast expanse of Arabian desert, and just north of this: the land of Syria. Back in Mesopotamia, at the central heart of it all: *Babylon – seat of the gods*.

---

5 Consider the archetypal past-time remaining in imaginative consciousness of building *sand-castles*.

6 Even the pathway of the rivers have changed over time with the creation of and then absence of human intervention via the aqueduct-canal systems and other natural occurrences.

Distinct natural terrain separates the Mesopotamian region into the northern and southern
parts, a factor exploited for political purposes.
Originally, southern *Sumer*[7] and northern *Akkad*
each were ruled by their own governors, called
a *patesi*.[8] With the post-Sumerian era unification of the two lands and the rise of the
Babylonian Empire, this figure was eventually
replaced by the *lugal*[9] – a title applied to the
"*Mighty King of both Sumer & Akkad*." The
northern half was once forested and so it retains
features of prairie and plains mixed with a
mountainous supply of stones and crystals. The
southern part is naturally more barren, essentially swamps and marshes mixed with arid
desert. Without the aid of the incredible
irrigation system employed, the *Babylonian
Empire* would never have had the freedom and
sustainability to survive and flourish as the
spiritual and political center of the ancient
world.

The city of Babylon was built alongside the

---

7   Also called (in varying texts): *Sumeria, Shinar,
    Babili, Babylonia* or *Chaldea*.

8   Usage of the title has been retained by the modern
    Mardukite Ministries to indicate a priest/minister-
    bishop of a particular region or diocese.

9   Literally: *lu* – man; *gal* – great or lofty. "Great Man."

western of the two rivers, the *Euphrates*.[10] It is considerably longer of the two rivers – at 1,800 miles – forming first in the heights of the mountains at 11,000 feet above sea level. It quickly drops off then falls approximately one foot per mile for the last 1,200 miles of its run. The pathway taken by the river has consistently moved westward with the absence of human intervention and canals – ceaselessly creating more area 'between' the rivers. The water levels are indicative of the equinoxes, like the Egyptian Nile,[11] with the *Euphrates* rising in the spring and lowering in the autumn.

Opposite the *Euphrates*, the broad eastern river runs 1,150 miles and, like the other, the path has also shifted to what archeologists believe to be its more 'natural' flow with the abandonment of the irrigation canals. The Greeks pronounce the Assyrian[12] name for the river as *Tigris*, essentially meaning "*serpent river*" although the original Sumerian[13] identification meant "*fast as an arrow.*" The Babylonians found the

---

10 Called *buranun* or *perath* by the Sumerians; *pu.rat.tu* (Assyrian), all meaning simply *river*.

11 Contrary to the Egyptian Nile, which is altered by the summer monsoon season, the *Euphrates* levels peak in the spring.

12 Babylonian/Assyrian – *i.di.ik.lat*

13 Sumerian – *idigna* or *id-dagal-la*

Tigris to be too 'wild' to cross easily or irrigate with, especially given the water levels rise and fall in direct opposition to the cycle of the *Euphrates*.[14]

Before emptying into the Persian Gulf, the *Euphrates* and *Tigris* actually join together[15] forming a marshy delta region called the "Great Swamp." The prehistoric city of Eridu was once a lavish capital at the coast of the Persian Gulf. Ruins and remains now rest 130 miles away from the sea. What has happened over time is attributed to the 'shrinking' of the Persian Gulf, creating more land – approximately *72 feet* of it *per* year!

What the *seeker* should note in comprehending this geographic overview is the ever-changing shape of the land, which was once expertly manipulated to meet the needs of an awe-inspiring civilization that went unparalleled. The proper cultivation of the land was the original key – making societal life possible among humans, and to this they attributed the knowledge to the *gods*, great sky beings, who not only taught the people how to best utilize

---

14 Cities founded alongside (and making use of) the *Tigris* include *Nineveh*, *Calah (Nimrud)* and *Asshur*.

15 Called the *Shatt al-'Arab*

the natural terrain, but they even reportedly did the hard part for them, shaping the land[16] and launching city-life for the sustenance of their own livelihood on earth. With the 'land between the rivers' prepared and consecrated, *kingship* could now be *lowered* from *heaven*.

---

16 "The *IGIGI-Watchers* dug the *Tigris River* and the *Euphrates* and opened canals to be the life of the land." – Mardukite Tablet-A Series, *Necronomicon Anunnaki Bible* edited by Joshua Free.

3. KINGSHIP FROM HEAVEN: DIVINE RIGHT

"Monarchy was the first form of government observed by man, and it was, according to almost every culture, created by God. It is the primordial, archetypal form of government, the most natural – that which all other forms of government vainly try to mimic, while at the same time violating its most basic tenets. For thousands of years before the modern era, when 90% of the population was not intellectually capable of participating in government or making electoral decisions, monarchy stood as the bulwark against the disintegration of the societal unit, providing a stability that otherwise could not be achieved. If monarchy had not been invented, human history could never have happened."

~ Tracy R. Twyman
Arcadian Mystique, 2005

An examination of the Sumerian and Babylonian *King-Lists*[17] will reveal the belief

17 Transliterated as the Mardukite K-Tablet Series,
   Necronomicon Anunnaki Bible edited by Joshua Free.

that "kingship" was "sent down" from "heaven" as decreed by the *gods*. To this we might add that a similar tradition has been followed by many indigenous ancient cultures.[18] These dynastic lists originate by Sumerian[19] hands, but they were later re-catalogued in Babylon by Nabu Priest-Scribes.[20] Similar *King-Lists* have also been found in Egypt[21] and they all suggest some very amazing notions for the contemporary mind to grasp.

The chronology of the *King-Lists* are separated by a critical event, one which is found within the cosmological records of all ancient cultures – the *Deluge* or *Great Flood*. This means that Sumerian civilization began in *antediluvian* times, prior to the *Deluge*. This controversial event consisted of both torrential storms and the rise of ground floor water in connection to the melting glaciers and ice at the end of the Pleist-

---

18 L.A. Waddell (in *Egyptian Civilization: Its Sumerian Origins*) suggests the same *King-Lists* appear in India.

19 The oldest Sumerian example being the *Weld-Blundell Prism* tablet.

20 Final Babylonian reconstruction and addendum provided by Berossus (c. 3rd century B.C.)

21 Known in Egypt as the *King-List* or *Dynastic Chronicles* catalogued by Manetho (c. 3rd century B.C.)

ocene[22] period. The *King-Lists* appear congruent with this time scale also, but the shifting sands of Mesopotamia provide few clues for us since the ancient sites were often dismantled or found in ruins and later built over by cultural successors. What this signifies is that the pre-Babylonian, pre-Sumerian *Ubaid*[23] periods are not the true absolute origins for "prehistoric" civilization, but instead the origins for the efforts that were resumed after the earth was stable for societal habitation again, following the last Ice Age.

Mystical texts speak of a "primordial sea" or "Abyss" that first swept over the earth (or in the universe) prior to the separation and manifestation of individual 'forms' in existence. Although it might be easy for a mythographer to simply attribute this archetypal image to a *Deluge*, all of the ancient records are in agreement that this was not the *first cause*, that *something* came before it, disagreeing only on a timeline and details.[24] Even the *Judeo-Christian*

---

22 Regarded by geologists as ending approximately 12,000 years *before present*.

23 Archeologists measure the *Ubaid* period based on the artistic styling used in pottery beginning 6,500 – 5,500 B.C.

24 Archeologists can successfully confirm the identities of the *King-Lists* until c. 3200 B.C., and they

texts support the idea that the *Deluge* took place *after* the creation of humans. But, further research will reveal that the entire Semitic scriptural basis for the *Deluge* and *Creationism* can be found practically verbatim on cuneiform tablets derived from thousands of years of tradition before the Semitic culture even existed unto itself. So, when asked – "Is it that the cuneiform tablets support the belief in *biblical* history or is the *Holy Bible* what lends credibility to the writings of greater antiquity?" – there is no 'good' answer because the question itself is at fault. There is, however, yet another significant similarity to address that would *appear* to unite the biblical beliefs with those of the more ancient cultures – returning us to our present topic on kingship.

Sumerian and Egyptian records are very clear about the nature of the being occupying the seat of kingship at its start – *gods*. The original *overseers* were considered *divine*, having come from the stars/sky and bringing with them the knowledge and technologies that would cultivate humanity. The reign of these *divine* be-

---

continue into the past for another 420,000+ years. By comparison, the Semitic belief is that the world as a whole was created in c. 4004 B.C., which would necessarily and incorrectly place the *Deluge* and other mythic events much more recent.

ings was eventually replaced by *hybrid demi-gods* (part-*Divine*; part-*human*) until finally being passed to the control of a specialized segment of mankind.[25] At each stage of development, the concept of *dynastic success-ion* remains paramount – the idea that the "divine blood" flows from the heart of the 'true' kings in the line, which in turn can be passed on to their offspring. The tradition of *Divine Right to Rule* is as ancient as human society altogether and may even have origins beyond only this planet.[26]

The origins of the word "ruler," "regent" and "realm" all reflect the absolute "god-like" nature of the original king, especially after the unification of the two lands of *Babylonia*, where one man – one *lugal* – was elevated to the position of a blessed and lofty *demigod.* More than simply a title of power, this role required

25 This is illustrated by the recorded length of reign on the *King-Lists*, first being 10's of thousands of years (*gods*), then hundreds of years (*demigods*) and finally more mortally realistic periods (*men*). In contrast, the Judeo-Christian scriptures reflect a similar concept in the subsequent lifespans of their own genealogies.

26 Cosmological tablets illuminate a similar tradition of *Divine Succession* practiced by the *Anunnaki* (sky gods), particularly *Anu, Enlil* and *Enki*, concerning the control of heavenly domains or celestial zones beyond earth.

the person to be an active intermediary between the people and the *gods* and thus acted as a kind of *priest-king*. What's more, the interconnectedness of the "realm" was inseparable from this king. The king and his land are one. The king and his people are one. The fate of one proved to reflect the other throughout history many times over and the people couldn't deny it – a good and just king resulted in expansion and fruitful land, whereas the rule of unjust ungodly tyrants weakened the integrity of the *Babylonian Empire* every time.

Properly guided kings realized they were essentially *Divine Representation* on earth and with this came great responsibility. In fact, the freedoms, responsibilities and penalties of the population all *rose* relative with class – quite different even, than what we see often today. The 'true' kings understood that they existed *for* the people, representatives of the *gods* on earth, exercising the same *divine power* that had been executed by the *gods* themselves in the cultivation of humanity. The descent of kingship come from the *gods of heaven* themselves, but is carried in the hearts of men – passing on genetic memory in the form of 'divine blood' installing the system known as *jure divino* – the episcopal law[27] upheld by one 'anointed' by *God*.[28]

Not wholly different than kingship, the 'social class system' has been in operation since the birth of societal civilization – possibly a inseparable aspect to monarchical programs. As with the matter of worldly reign mixed with the *human condition*, the issue of 'social class' has been handled with more care during some periods of history as opposed to others. During the rule of Khammurabi in Babylon, there were three distinct classes: *Amelum*, *Mushkinu* and *Wardum*. The *Amelum* consisted of the highest orders of kings, priests, court officials and governors. The largest of the classes was the *Mushkinu*, made up of the average citizen or worker, with certain social rights to protect loss or limb. Be-neath all of these were the slave-*wardums* who were not only provided shelter in their master's house but also granted a mate.[29] Contrary to the more eastern traditions, class

---

27 From the Greek *episkopos*, meaning – *overseer*.

28 A similar belief attributed to the *laying of hands* is carried in the Catholic Church concerning the succession of the power of the *Holy Spirit* that is passed on to the clergy, allegedly descended from the biblical Peter, the first apostolic pope.

29 The temples and local governments owned the largest number of slave-workers.

was not necessarily fixed for one's lifetime – the *wardum* could potentially purchase their own freedom in time.

4. BABYLONIAN HISTORY:
A SYNTHESIS

"Since Marduk created me to be king and Nabu has culled his people to my realm – as the love I have for my own life, so do I feel toward the building and reign of their cities."

~ Nebuchadnezzar II
Mardukite Tablet-L Series,
Necronomicon Anunnaki Bible

The oldest capital city of the proto-Uruk Sumerians is *Eridu*,[30] dated to c. 5500 B.C. – over seven thousand years ago. Pre-Babylonian tablets of the Sumerians indicate that the site, sacred to the *Anunnaki god*, *Enki*, was actually restored and rebuilt many times in history.[31] Curiously, Assyriologists have misappropriated what they call "The *Oldest* Creation Myth" to

---

30 Eridu is derived from the Sumerian – *e-ri-dug* or *uru-du(g)*, the present-day site: *Tell abu Shahrain*.

31 The divine mythos of Mesopotamia, focused on the *Anunnaki*, attributes Eridu as the place of antediluvian kings, meaning that it was simply re-established after the *Deluge* and may even serve as the origins of the *Atlantis*-archetype that is ingrained in human consciousness.

Eridu, actually naming it the *Eridu Genesis* – though it was not found in Eridu and it does not represent a true cosmology, but merely one part of the *Deluge*-cycle.[32] What Eridu *was* most famous for, aside from its antiquity, was the first temple *ziggurat*, the E.Abzu – *Enki's Sea Tower*, now in ruins.

In addition to being the place where kingship was first "lowered" from "heaven" under the decree of the *Anunnaki*, the later classical renderings by Berossus allude to Eridu as the *prototype* of *Babilu* (Babylon), being the original cite of the *Gate of the Gods*. Later duplication attempts were then made in Babylon with the rise of the ancient Mardukites, consequently becoming the proverbial *Tower of Babel*. To remain concise, this present text will remain restricted to that which immediately pertains to *Babylonia*,[33] however, as with the geography and other offered details, a thorough background is critical for the modern *seeker* to fully grasp this foreign and chronologically dis-

---

32 The *Eridu Genesis* was excavated from Nippur and is dated to only c. 1800 B.C.

33 A previous treatise, *Sumerian Religion* by Joshua Free, also known as Mardukite *Liber 50*, offers extensive details on the prehistoric 'Sumerian Anunnaki' prior to (and leading up to) the Babylonian systematization.

tant aspect of history – *the legacy of Babylon*.

Prior to the establishment of Mardukite Babylon, most of the activity of the Uruk[34] Sumerians was concentrated in the southern parts of Mesopotamia, now using *Eridu* as its secondary capital, after the city of Uruk (Erech). An adequate opening made way for the evolution of Mesopotamia when control of the region,

---

34 Post-Ubaid Sumerian period generally catagorized as
   c. 3250 – 2700 B.C.

and the privilege of executing *Divine Right*, fell under dispute between two *patesis* – Urukagina of Lagash[35] and Lugal-Zaggisi of Umma. Urukagina was a social reformer popular among the people, but he could not successfully hold back the militant efforts of the Umma. Using the 'short chronology'[36] version of dating adopted by archeologists, the hold of the Umma was relinquished in c. 2600 B.C.[37] by Sargon, the founder of the Akkadian Dynasty[38] – the Semitic faction north of Sumer.

Sargon of Akkad (*Sharru-Kin*) is often confused by amateurs[39] with another Babylonian king sh-

---

35 Both a township and a dynasty, Lagash was home to the *Temple of Fifty* – E.Ninnu – sacred to the *Anunnaki god* Ninurta.

36 Based on the dating of Khammurabi's reign to the 1700's B.C. as opposed to an older period alluded to that often adds between 500 and 1,000 years (or more) to accepted dates of events.

37 The texts developed by the later scribes of Nabunidus indicate c. 3750 B.C.

38 It should be understood that while the political 'seat of power' moves from place to place through history (and does not even always include the city of Babylon until more recent post-Sumerian ages), the origination and continuation of the individual dynasties exist independent of one another, whether or not they are actually recognized as 'currently' *in* power.

39 This would undoubtedly have proposed issues for the

aring the same name, Sargon II, the Assyrian who appears on the scene nearly two-thousand years later during the *Neo-Babylonian Empire*. Sargon's son Rimush (c. 2580 B.C.) reigns after his father's death and becomes the self-proclaimed *King of Kish* – a title which cost him his life. After his murder, his brother Manishtusu replaces him, during which the Elamites[40] revolt. His son, Naram-Sin, named himself the *King of the Four Quarters* and successfully conquered the Magan[41] lands among others. He wrongfully did so in the name of the *gods* and as punishment, the rapid expansion caused the heart of his empire to weaken. When the dynasty of Sargon was replaced by the Enlilite Gutians (c. 2450 B.C.), their reign was rejected and political confusion swept over the region until a new acceptable dynasty could be established.

The new dynasty came again from Lagash. Of the *patesi* in that line the most influential include Urbau, who expanded the power of the

---

original Assyriologists in charge of plotting the cultural chronology for science.

40 *Elamites* – pro-Ninurta Persians, named for (biblical) Shem's son, Elam. Proto-Elamites emerge c. 3200 B.C. but their capital, Susa, founded c. 5000 B.C.

41 Located on the Arabian peninsula, separating *Babylonia* from Egypt.

E.Ninnu in Lagash as well as many other religious centers; and Gudea brought abundance and prosperity to the lands by opening and securing trade routes. With the death of Gudea's son, Ur-Dingirsu, no heir was brought forth and the dynastic line ended (c. 2250 B.C.) allowing the 'seat of power' to be passed to the city (and "third dynasty") of Ur,[42] led by Ur-Engur (Ur-Nammu) who focused on the fortification of the Babylonian infrastructure and the reinstatement of the 'glory' of Enlil. His son, Dungi (better known as Shulgi), called himself the *High Priest of* Anu, then reinforced the importance of the Eridu site and the legacy of Enki. But there is much more to this part of the story.

The patronage toward the *Anunnaki god* Nanna-Sin was the result of a 'life-debt owed' when the *god* personally arranged the marriage between Ur-Nammu and 'a high priestess of the temple of Ur.' In the balance of this, the dynasty of Ur sought a truly 'Sumerian' Renaissance, which fought hard to thwart the advancement of the pro-Mardukites. Although economic and agricultural abundance was found under this reign, the uprisings and social rebellions sparked by

---

42 *Ur* – patron city of the *Anunnaki god* Nanna-Sin; significant ziggurat temple remains at modern site: *Tell el-Muqayyar.*

this 'new' movement grew rather than diminish-ed. Shulgi also becomes a 'lover' to the *Anunnaki goddess queen* Inanna-Ishtar, and under her blessing he begins to fight the Nabu-tribes (ancient Mardukites) c. 2095 B.C., a task passed down to his son, Amar-Sin,[43] a warlord king who unleashed vengeance on all (Mardukite) rebels. War ensues between 2048 and 2024 B.C. which results in the unleashing of nuclear weapons (born of *alien* knowledge) against the pro-Marduk westerners.[44]

The Amorites[45] were essentially a Semitic people, centralized on the city of Mari in Syria.[46] Although they were, by nature, particip-

---

43 Also known as Amar-Pal; or in Hebrew – *Amraphel, King of Sumer* [Genesis 14]

44 See *End of Days* by Zecharia Sitchin.

45 *Amorites* – Akkadian term *Amurru* refers to this culture, geography and language; Sumerian – (A)Mar.Tu. Curiously, according to the *Book of Jubilees* (a Judeo-*Enlilite* text also known as the *Leptogenesis*) "The former *giants*, the *Rephaim*, gave way to the *Amorites*, an evil and sinful people whose wickedness surpasses that of any other, and whose life will be cut short on earth."

46 The city of Mari (one of many cult centers for Inanna-Ishtar) occupies present-day Syria; modern site – *Tell Hariri*; but the Amorite rebels that joined the pro-Marduk movement also occupied the Arabian desert just west of the Euphrates during the *Third*

ants in the cult-worship of Inanna-Ishtar, their position against the Neo-Sumerian Empire of Ur was key to the later rise of a true *Mardukite Babylon*, even if only at its initial height for a short time. This monumental period dedicated to the power and splendor that is Babylon, was instilled by a Semitic dynasty[47] (c. 2057 B.C.) that would include the famous Khammurabi.[48] But then, after Khammurabi's death, the Babylonian dynasty was broken by the Hittites[49] (c. 1950 B.C.) followed by a series of mysterious "sea-kings" (c. 1850 B.C.) that spawn an additional (second) Babylonian dynasty.

When the *Old Babylonian* age had ended, the loose organization and broken political structure of the empire left the lands open for a new dyn-

---

Dynasty of Ur.

47 Often referred to be historians and scholars as the *First Semitic Dynasty of Babylon*.

48 Who ironically sacked the rebellious city of Mari for its anti-Marduk cult worship of Inanna-Ishtar.

49 *Hittites* – mentioned often as adversaries in Egyptian literature; emerging from the Black Sea region and Taurus Mountains, later referred to as the "Land of the Hittites" (or *Antolia*). They assimilate Sumerian mythos but are not Sumerian; just as the later Assyrians adopt the Babylonian traditions but were not themselves. Hittites were famous for the first military use of chariots. Biblical scholars count them among the *Canaanites*.

astic power change by, fortunately, a pro-Marduk force known as the Kassites[50] (c. 1750 B.C.) who had formed and come down from the Zagros Mountain region northeast of *Babylonia*. The Kassites assimilated Marduk with their own deity-name, *Shuqamuna*[51] and defended a Mardukite Babylon against years of struggle with the Hittites who sought to reclaim *Babylonia* for themselves. Apart from this, the Kassites were a diplomatic people who enjoyed trade relations with most of the known world. Unique to their time of reign was a spiritual revolution in Egypt under Amonhotep IV (Akhenaton) where the *Marduk-Aten-Ra Star Religion* (Mardukite) was being ignited. Significant correspondence (c. 1350 B.C.) was exchanged between Egypt and at least two Kassite Kings – Kadashman Khar-loe I and Burnaburiash II.[52] But this is not the only peculiarly unique event to have transpired during the rule of the Kassites.

In 1595 B.C.[53], the Hittites successfully enter

---

50 "Third" or Kassite Dynasty of Babylon.
51 Possibly derived from the more eastern nomenclature
   – *Shakyamuni* – or Buddha.
52 Called the *Amarna Letters* – some 400 found at
   Akhenaton's capital city in Egypt, all in Akkadian
   cuneiform, not Egyptian.
53 Some sources also suggest 1651 B.C. depending on
   the chronology accepted.

Babylon and 'steal' Marduk. Historians will usually interpret this to mean that they 'removed the image of Marduk' from the temple, signifying the main statue or 'idol' that represented the 'seat of power' in Babylon. Other literalists will conclude that the *Anunnaki god* himself was actually captured. In either case, the Kassites devote over two decades in battle toward recovering and returning it (him) to the temple. In spite of the struggles with the Hittites, the Kassite Dynasty maintains its reign of Babylon, with few minor exceptions, for nearly half of a millennium.

By the end of their rule, the Kassites primary issues were no longer with the Hittites, but instead with a rising force from the east, *Elam*. They replace the Mesopotamian dynasties with their own for a time and also succeed in stealing to their city of Susa a relic from Babylon – the *stele* on which the *Code of Khammurabi*[54] was written. But sovereignty in *Mardukite Babylonia* seems to pass to those *most able*, as the salvation of the land would require the 'Eye and

---

54 Also called the *Law of Marduk*, to replace the preexisting Sumerian *Code of Ur-Nammu*. Analytical scholars find them to be almost identical in pragmatic nature; the primary difference being one of 'divine politics' – the *Anunnaki deity* names credited with the worldly law and order being exercised.

Hand of Marduk' to pass to foreigners in hopes of launching a *Neo-Babylonian* empire – the "Fourth Dynasty of Babylon"[55] (c. 1200 B.C.), the 'Assyrian' dynasty including Nabuchadnezzar I[56] who recovered the *stele* from the Elamites (c. 1125 B.C.). However, the efforts toward a *Neo-Babylonian* empire were quickly thwarted by Ara-means and several small short-lived dynasties.

A Mardukite emphasis returns to *Babylonia* by way of Nabu-mukin-apli (c. 1000 B.C.) and during this, Babylon's "eighth" dynasty, significant efforts are made to restore temples and statuary is refinished in gold and lapis, leading the population toward a true *Babylonian Renaissance*. However, during this time, the Babylonians have frequent issues with the uprising western Sutu-tribes[57], who at times prevented the religio-political festival ceremonies from occurring proper.[58] During this

---

55 Dynastic *patesi*, Marduk-Shapik-Zeri campaigns to reunite the lands.

56 Assyrian – Nabu-kudurri-usur.

57 *Sutu* – Nomadic Enlilite desert tribe of Aramaeans who patron Adad (or Haddad, the storm god), Nanna-Sin and Ishtar.

58 Particularly the transfer (ceremonial procession) of the Nabu 'statue' from Borsippa to be united with Marduk's 'statue' in Babylon during the Spring

struggle, Nabu-apla-iddina[59] (in Babylon) works to maintain as much peace with his rivals as possible, including the Assyrian king, Ashur-nasipal II.[60]

The Ninth Dynasty of Babylon included the famous Nabu-nasir (c. 750 B.C.),[61] as well as Nabu-nadin-zeri (c. 735 B.C.), who was killed during a riot; and Nabu-suma-ukin II (c. 732 B.C.), who was replaced after one month by an Aramaen chief, Nabu-mukin-zeri, who was killed in a siege of Babylon by the Assyrians by Tiglath-Pileser III.[62] In c. 720 B.C., the throne is

Equinox (*A.ki.ti*) festival. Though it may have become a ceremonial observance involving statuary, this and many other traditions were based on the original actions of the *Anunnaki gods* themselves when they identifiably 'walked' among the people of earth.

59 Launches a literary *Renaissance* by reviving the Order of the Nabu priest-scribes; the salvaging and recopying of older cuneiform tablets of spirito-religious, political, astronomical or scientific use.

60 Nabu-apla-iddina forms a peace treaty with Shalmanesar II, son of Ashurnasipal II.

61 Nabonassar c. 747 B.C. begins the *Babylonian Chronicle*, event recording by scribe-priests beginning with his reign – dating system "AN" (*Anno Nabonassan*) integrated during Nabonassar Era.

62 Founder of the Tenth Dynasty of Babylon, the *Neo-Assyrian Empire* (c. 730 B.C.)

assumed by a Chaldean prince, Marduk-apla-iddina II[63] who struggles for control of Babylon against Sargon II. At one juncture, Sargon II succeeds in driving him away from Babylon for over a decade, but after Sargon's death, Marduk-apla-iddina II resumes power of the throne and succeeds in sparking revolution in *Babylonia* before dying in exile (c. 700 B.C.), forcing the region into political confusion for a time.

Following the fall of Assyrian power with the death of Ashurbanipal (c. 630 B.C.), the Babylonians elect a leader of the revolution, Nabopolassar[64] as king. He then joins forces with the Chaldeans and Medes in fighting and defeating the Assyrians at their capital of Nineveh (c. 612 B.C.) and later the Egyptians. Aging and war-warn after successful victories against two empires, he passed the power of the throne to his son while still alive. His son: the famous Nabuchadnezzar II (c. 600 B.C.)[65] sup-

---

63 The biblical *Merodach-Baladan*.

64 Akkadian – *Nabu-apal-usur*.

65 He is credited with the construction of the "Hanging Gardens in Babylon" and many other acts supporting the Mardukite Renaissance, calling himself in one tablet inscription: *Nabu's Favorite*. The "Hanging Gardens" were allegedly a present for his Median (Persian) wife to remind her of her native lands.

ported a pro-Marduk era for fifty years, with the unification of Sumer and Akkad in the name of Marduk and Nabu. He restored many city centers and *ziggurats*, though before his death, he predicted an impending end to the glory of his Chaldean Empire in Babylon. The actions of the rulers who were his successors, invariably proved him right.

The heir to Nabuchadnezzar II was Awel-Marduk (c. 560 B.C.)[66], who only reigned for two years before his death – but he had usurped the throne against the will of his father, who was still in power. Awel-Marduk was murdered by his brother-in-law and successor Nergal-sharezer, whose name and actions indicated his assistance to the 'true' king, Nabuchadnezzar II. Any short-lived reform efforts to maintain the integrity of *Babylonia* were quickly dissolved by one of the most unjust anti-Marduk kings (c. 555 B.C.) in an otherwise *Mardukite Renaissance*.

After the death of Nabuchadnezzar II, the 'Seat of Babylon' was usurped by the Assyrian who called himself "Nabonidus," meaning *Nabu is exalted*, though his suppression of the Marduk-ites, desecration of holy sites and violation of

---

66 Or – *Amel-Marduk*, also called *Evil Merodach*.

countless traditions would dictate he lived my another creed. In fact, he had fallen pray to the 'cult of the moon god'[67] in lieu of the sun and stellar traditions and actually forbid the Mardukite *Akiti* (or *Akitu*) "New Year" festival of the spring equinox from taking place. To prevent the utter annihilation of his people, the "Eye and Hand of Marduk" must again fall upon foreigners. Cyrus the Great marches on Babylon and rightfully dethrones Nabonidus, sparking the Persian Dynasty of Babylon. He attributes all of his success in this venture to the power of the *Anunnaki god* Marduk.[68] His dynasty is allowed to continue until the arrival of the Greek Hellenistic Dynasty by Alexander the Great in 330 B.C.

---

67 The 'lunar-cult' is usually associated with the *Anunnaki god* Nanna-Sin, and by definition Enlilite in nature – it is generally attributed to the pre-Babylonian traditions of the Uruk Sumerians who were also devoted to the *Anunnaki goddess* Inanna-Ishtar.

68 See "*Capture of Babylon with the Favor of Marduk*," Tablet-L Series, *Necronomicon Anunnaki Bible* edited by Joshua Free.

5. CUNEIFORM – BIRTH OF THE SYSTEMS

"The education of the Babylonians was entirely in the hands of the priests, who derived their knowledge from Nabu, the inventor of writing and letters, and every kind of learning – the Lord of "Houses of Tablets" (or books), i.e. libraries."

~ E.A. Wallis Budge
Babylonian Life & History, 1925

The overt evolution of the Sumerians into a *Babylonian Empire* is, as we have displayed in the prior section on history, not altogether surprising – on the surface. However, the *seeker* should keep in perspective just how quickly all of this developed from seemingly nothing. It is true that societal living was originally organized around *state religion*, but prior to this it was culminated not by the social relationships shared between people, but by their living relationship with the earth. Where first we have loosely organized nomadic hunter-gatherers that are forced to wander about or dwell in caves, essentially rolling the dice of chance for their survival, very little time passes before the sweeping transition in Mesopotamia toward planned agricultural farming and pasturing shepherds.

According to the ancient tablets, the decision to cultivate civilization in the *Middle East* was not of men, but of a genetically distinct race known as the *Anunnaki* – those that 'came down from the sky' and were later called the *gods* of the original 'pantheon' of deities on earth. These tablets[69] also describe the originating purpose behind the 'genetic upgrade' of humanoids on the planet to make them fit to be workers for the *gods*. This began prior to what we call the *Deluge* and was still under the direction of 'divine' *overseers*, not yet the mortal priest-kings found in the more popular chronicles – thus not yet truly 'human' civilization. With the rule of men, believing themselves to be *gods*, the 'seat' of power shifts frequently throughout history – as frequently as the whims and devotions of humans change.

Anunnaki control of the 'heavens' and 'aero-space' rested with the *god* Anu and his son En-

---

69 See "*Creation and Disposal of Men*," Mardukite Tablet-G Series, *Necronomicon Anunnaki Bible* edited by Joshua Free.

lil, respectively. The material world, however – the realm most integrated with human life – became the domain of another son of Anu, named Enki.[70] Although the majority of ancient Mesopotamia became classified as *Enlilite* territory, the origins of the systematic 'arts' of civilization emerge from Enki's southern city of Eridu on the coast of the Persian Gulf. It is here that we find the origins of true 'human' civilization, born not out of innate necessity or simple survival – but through the condition-ing of the psyche with the integration of 'worldly' *systems*. The means by which this as executed on earth among humans – the *written word*.

Historians credit the Sumerians with many 'firsts' in civilization. The more pragmatic elements of their urban survival; irrigation, pasturing, roads, the wheel. . . all contribute to the surface reality that archeologists are restricted to in their findings. In Mesopotamia, however, the findings quickly become primarily of a different nature – *clay tablets*. Much like the Egyptians using hieroglyphics, the early Su-

---

70 *Enki* – meaning: Lord (*En*) of the Earth (*Ki*), applied to the *Anunnaki god* named "E.A." in Sumerian – meaning: *Dweller in the Deep*.

merian cuneiform[71] writing was equally a tradition of 'picture' writing[72] etched with sticks and
fingernails. The refinement of the writings continued throughout the pre-Babylonian *Sumerian*
age, but in c. 2100 B.C., the form changed
dramatically with a gift of Nabu for his scribe-
priests – the reed *stylus* pen.

This monumental cornerstone in human development is the very reason we have the vast
tablet collections available today by which we
are able to glean this incredible and forgotten
empire.

Those who are easily dismissive of our current
subject matter (in this book), or simply find
topics of the tablets drawn from the *Ancient
Near East* to be boring and without relevance,
have most likely never had the explanation
given to them proper – that this emphasis on

---

71 *Cuneiform* – form the Latin *cuneus* meaning: wedge.
72 Sumeriologist, L.A. Waddell, believes that the
   Egyptian hieroglyphics and early Sumerian
   cuneiform share similar origins. The use of both also
   seems to occur synchronous with one another
   chronologically in time, with the Egyptians only
   marginally trailing behind the Sumerians – similar to
   the way culture had been imported to the east cost of
   the U.S. and took some time to migrate to the west
   coast (and sometimes vice-versa).

'words' is why things *are* the way they *are* even to this day. Early picture writing was sufficient for many things, particularly given the simplicity of the goals during its usage, primarily *survival*. Hunting grounds, natural dangers and even some elaborate stories could all be marked with a primitive 'picture' language. Communication between humans themselves became easy enough to navigate using speech and gesture, so what was the purpose of writing? – of *words that stay?*[73]

All of the forthcoming dependent *systems* on the planet, those that create the 'elevated' social network of the human animal, relied on the relay of the written word to be effective. With the creation of the *stylus*, this was possible – and a methodology for *systems* was relayed among the masses. The success of this, mainly to aid in the *Anunnaki* 'control' of an exponentially growing human population, is then really a composite of two efforts: the birth of *systems* in Eridu by Enki (with the aid of, not surprisingly, his heir-son Marduk),[74] but also the ratification

---

73 In the 1980's classic motion picture *The Dark Crystal*, young Jen defines *writing* as 'words that stay.'

74 Of little attention in pre-Babylonian literature and tradition, Marduk is the original *High Priest of Enki* in *Eridu*, the birthplace of religion, magic and other

of writing by Nabu much later, which enabled these *systems* to be activated in *Babylonia*.

The human psyche then became conditioned to societal living, itself now connecting two aspects internally: *pictures* and *words*. The two had already been 'one' in form – as picture writing, but only in the vaguest sense. The use of the *stylus* changed all this by not only speeding up the flow and form of the written images, but as a straight-edged tool, this pen eliminated the 'curvature' of the characters. No longer would someone need (or be able) to draw out the image of several animals to depict them, a series of quick hashed-wedge marks could be used in its stead – and in the human consciousness, the two would become inseparable in meaning.[75] Now, this certainly was not evolut-

societal systems.

75 The solidification of abstract concepts and ideas represented by words actually changes the way the brain thinks – changes the way in which one experiences these aspects of reality. Likewise, the adoption of a label system for fixed nouns and names creates an internal database called a 'schema' which also manipulates experiences and memory. The only experimentation psychologists and anthropologists have had at their disposal for this is the perceptual comparison of the western individual with a more 'aboriginal' one still active today. The general consensus has been that these perceptions are

ionarily necessary for the survival of the species, but for the survival of the *system*, by which matters of commerce and state, laws and government, roles and order, religion and trade could all be *fixed* to writing, securing the imprinted history and fate of the human consciousness to *words that stay.*

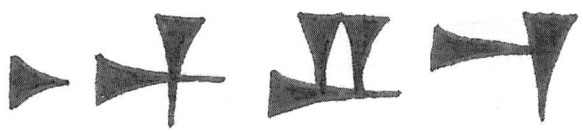

"*ilu-Na-Bu*" / god-NABU

The cuneiform-wedge writing system is actually quite different than the more recently used classical alphabets. In fact, it really is not an alphabet[76] at all, but a series of symbols to represent phonetic syllable sounds – combinations of a consonant and a vowel. Thus, we have no real available form for a singular letter *B*, but there are signs for *ab*, *ib*, *ub*, *ba*, *be*, *bi* and *bu*.

A refined *stylus*-based cuneiform coupled with the ease of clay tablet construction developed

---

evolutionarily advantages to the environment that the individual is reared to.

76 Although scholars have created correspondences between it and other later (derived) Semitic alphabets such as Hebrew to aid them in translation.

into a plethora of written records in the ancient world.[77] By c. 2000 B.C., the Babylonian laws required that all transactions be documented and duplicated – sometimes even *triplicated* – by official *scribe-priests*.[78] The necessity and invention of the *cylinder-seal* came into being, a clay signature-seal that was uniquely fashioned for an individual and often worn or carried like a large bead. This could be 'rolled' across the tablet surface to create a rectangular stamp-mark. And just to be sure there was no tampering, the Nabu scribe-priests even developed a unique way of enclosing and preserving a signed clay tablet within a clay envelope that contained a duplicated signed inscription on the

---

77 Eventually, a 'royal library' was established in *Babylonia* as a Temple of Nabu, maintained by the official librarian-priest known as a *Rab Girginakki* in Akkadian (according to Budge). Efforts to create and preserve 'archival libraries' later occurred in other places in Mesopotamia – always under the direction of the 'current' *authority* in power.

78 For an exceptionally long period of human history, only the higher classes of citizen were required to learn reading and writing and thus the dependency on the scribe-priests among the common masses became great. Any discovered indiscretion or falsehoods relayed in this process were severely punished, which strengthened the faith of the people in these 'life-depending' records and deeds of ownership.

outside.[79] This gave rise to the original form of banking and commerce – trading in kind, complete with a notarized receipt. In addition, a new *system* of conceptual wealth could be integrated as well: the possession of land property – or *real estate* – which was authorized and governed by the state.

The installation and development of the 'human world' (in the fashion just described) included one additional facet with a role that was not so obvious to the common man – and certainly not to early *Assyriologists*: the covert governing body that had originally dictated these *systems* into being and initially regulated the means in which they were integrated into social consciousness. Such might be easily overlooked or taken for granted by the contemporary mind and yet it is entirely connected to where humans are, were and will be. Definitions, semantics, boundaries and the ability to record them into histories, calendars, maps, property deeds and even shopping lists – that will *remain* and be *understood* for future generations – completely and utterly changed the experience of human existence in the universe.

---

79 In special circumstances an additional copy would be retained by the archivist.

MARDUKITE

6. NABU & THE SECRET SOCIETY OF BABYLON

"The Palace of Ashurbanipal, King of the World, King of Assyria, who in Assur and Belit puts his trust, on whom Nabu and Tasmitu have bestowed broad ears, who has acquired clear eyes. The valued products of the scribe's art, such as no one among the kings who has gone before me had acquired, the wisdom of Nabu, unequaled, as so much as can be found, I have had inscribed on tablets and arranged in groups. I have revised, and for the sign of my reading, have set in my Palace this library – I, the ruler, who knows the Light of Assur, the King of the Gods."

~ Ashurbanipal (c. 700 B.C.)
Dedication of the Royal Library

What scholars now term 'Babylonian Mythology' is actually an evolution of the Sumerian legacy[80] in time and space, the progression of a particular *Anunnaki* family in Mesopotamia and *not* simply the assimilation or application to a

---

80 See *Sumerian Religion* by Joshua Free – a.k.a.
Mardukite Liber 50 or *Gates of the Necronomicon*.

similar pantheon – as we see in the later classical mythoi that simply regurgitate to us the ancient themes with new names. Therefore, the Babylonian religious and political pantheon should be viewed as an extension of the older Sumerian one.[81] In this case, however, the focus is transferred to a 'younger generation' of *Anunnaki gods*, as 'sealed' in the Babylonian Tradition.

The position of the 'heavenly father' (turned 'grandfather' by the younger generation) held by Anu[82] remains unchallenged. The emphasis, however, turns to more worldly concerns – for control of the position of 'earthly father' of the local universe[83], a title bestowed to Enlil, the royal heir of Anu, according to Sumerian tradition. Enlil's heir is his own royal son, Ninurta, and so the succession of the line was set to continue, making the earth a global *Enlilite* nation. Although Enki was given the charge as 'Lord of the Earth'[84], the division between the roles of Enlil and Enki blur. In Sumerian times

---

81 Giving rise to many misconceptions and misunderstandings by interpreters of the tablets of varying origins.

82 Which carries with it the numerical designation of 60 – the perfect number in Sumerian tradition.

83 Given the numerical designation of 50.

84 Given the numerical designation of 40.

they aid one another in the foundation of the material world, but by the Babylonian age, each has their own dedicated following among the population – essentially splitting the human race into dualism.[85]

With the evolution of the cuneiform writing, the face of the religion changed into the more familiar versions of Mesopotamia mythologies that it is defined by today. In pre-Babylonian Sumer, the temple-shrines simply acted as the earth-homes of the respective deity that it was dedicated to and the priests were intermediaries bet-ween the population and the *god*. The implementation of *writing* being brought, the mystical and religious tablets could now be created to not only solidify and protect the traditions, but actually *manipulate* them. This primitive logic became the basis for most of the *systems* even still active today.

85 According to the early Babylonian versions, this division occurred first concerning the genetic upgrade of humanity and then over the 'disposal' of the human race during the *Deluge*. Enlil, an *Anunnaki* nationalist, high commander and heir to Anu, is understandably reserved toward the creation and assistance of humanity. Enki, the chief scientist and magician of the *Anunnaki*, with a dynastic line that is not granted the same royal distinction as Enlil, sees potential in the human race to preserve his own legacy and that of his son, Marduk.

In short – reality is based on the experience of the *realm*, the world of light that we see and acknowledge stimuli from. The world of light is separated into *forms*, which require *classification* as 'things' within a coherent *system* to carry any semantic or 'conceptual' meaning as a functioning *program*.[86] Given that the basis of writing is to collect 'data', the interpretation in consciousness equates it to *facts*. Thus, the *words that stay* are *facts* collected about *reality* to enable the processing of cohesive *experience*. Here we find too, historical tablets of the deeds of kings and even cosmological tablets of the deeds of gods and the *beliefs* about *reality* become dictated for the population and presented as *facts*. Conclusively,[87] from the vantage point of the human condition, the *written word dictates reality*.[88]

The *Mardukite* priests of Babylon were, by nature, *Priests of Enki*, following a derivative of the ancient *systems* born in Eridu. Beyond the *collected data* to support a belief system, the

---

86 This is what enables even the current author to write *words* and have a reader comprehend them.

87 Q.E.D.

88 To be fair, while men and kings have gone to their graves each believing in their own truth, these thousands of years later, it is the *written word* from their era that has survived them all.

first pragmatic mystical and religious use of writing was the recording of *incantations*. An examination of these[89] reveals them to be essentially *appeals* to the *gods* for assistance in material matters. This became more *figurative* in time as the temple-shrine *ziggurat*-homes of the *Anunnaki gods* themselves became occupied instead by worldly representatives of the same.

Originally, people were instructed to petition their needs to the temple-priests, who would in turn make the appropriate offerings and incantations to the deity involved.[90] This represents a distinction between the 'surface' *system*-religion of the public population and the religious practices (traditions) of the scribe-priests, temple-priests and king-priests themselves.[91] Although *Mardukite* Babylon was hardly ruled by Mar-

---

89 Extensive tablet incantations appear transliterated throughout the Mardukite works, specifically the *Necronomicon Anunnaki Bible* and the Mardukite *Liber 50*, best known to the public as *Sumerian Religion* by Joshua Free.

90 This *system* is still installed in society today – in both religion and politics – where ministers and authorities act as intermediaries between the lay-person or common citizen and the perceptibly 'higher powers'.

91 The three 'classes' of *priest* in *Babylonia* – scribe, temple and king – where the *scribes* research and write the tablets, the *temple-priests* enact the tablets and the *kings* enforce the tablets.

duk's own lineage – all of *Babylonia* was still maintained under his care by way of the priest-kings who were nearly all under the influence of a prestigious secret society that changed the shape of Mesopotamia and the later world with nearly two millennium of unbroken covert operation in *Babylonia*: the *Priests of Nabu*.

Nabu is an enigmatic figure in history. He is ranked[92] among the Babylonian hierarchy of *Anunnaki gods*, as heir-son to Marduk's dynasty,[93] born of Sarpanit[94] – making him both earth-born and little more than half-divine. The name '*Nabu*'[95] indicates a "herald" or "announcer" and was eventually integrated into the Semitic-Hebrew language (as *nabih*) to mean "prophet." By the time of *Classical Mardukite Babylon*[96] (c. 2150 B.C.) his temple-city and

---

92 Given the numerical designation of 12 – indicative of cycles, time, knowledge and magic.

93 Thought to be shared by a brother (possibly a rival) Sutu (also Satu or Sati), whose name means *mountain* or *life of the mountain*. Another possible 'half-brother' and 'rival' is listed as Asar. This dynastic family also appears in Egypt under varying names.

94 An earth-born human wife taken by Marduk, who was actually descended from Adapa, the first human genetically upgraded by Enki.

95 Meaning literally: *who speaks for*.

96 Corresponding with the end of the *Old Kingdom* in Egypt and the launch of the 'royal' *Dragon Court* by

cult center was localized near Babylon at Borsi-ppa.[97] Having been also given the title '*Tutu*',[98] Nabu replaces the previous agricultural goddess of the Sumerian tradition, Nisaba.[99] This reflects the more '*druidic*' side of Nabu, being also a 'nature-deity' who is called upon to bless the crops and land for fertility.

It could be said, particularly in relation to the surviving tablets from this period, that Nabu represents the epit-ome of the "*pen is mightier than the sword.*" Where the previous *Anunnaki gods* had already cultivated civilization with their contributions – the *cattle and grain* had already been brought, the *pickax* had already been given[100] – Nabu offers the *reed stylus* and

---

Ankhfn-khonsu (c. 2170 B.C.).

97 Sumerian – *Bad.si(a).ab.ba(ki)*; Akkadian – *Bar-sip*; Present-day site of *birs-i-nimrud*.

98 An obscure title, rarely equated by scholars to the solar deity called Utu (Sumerian) or Shammash (Akkadian); the ancient root *tu* means to weave or integrate; the University of Pennsylvania cuneiform database lists the definition of *tu-tu* as "to approach or withstand" equated to *maharu* in Akkadian, meaning: "to confront or oppose."

99 Who is acknowledged in the Sumerian tradition as providing the initial pictorial system of writing, but this may be figurative and political only as she lives coinciding with the age of Gilgamesh.

100 See Mardukite *Liber 50*, released to the public as

reformation of the cuneiform writing system, which with it sparks the revived interest in the arts of Eridu – the divination, magic and science of Enki and Marduk, which can now be systematized for public installation. In post-Sumerian records, Nabu is also the guardian of the *Tablets of Destiny*,[101] that which sealed material creation to the *Divine Right* of the *Anunnaki*.

The magic and mysticism[102] of *Babylonia* was mainly restricted to the priests and was wholly religious in nature – rooted in the power and technologies of the *gods*. Any ancient "occult" or "magickal" texts from this age are primarily hymns and prayers. What might later serve as doctrines or scriptures, originated as historical documents among the Mesopotamians chronicling creation and universal order, the genesis of man, the flood cycle and the eventual restoration of civilization.[103] The forging and

---

Sumerian Religion (or *Gates of the Necronomicon*) by Joshua Free.

101 Possibly singular – a cuneiform tablet document ensuring Enlilship of the local universe (earth), sometimes referred to as a *me*, which are usually circular inscribed with divine decrees (world order).

102 Born in Eridu, then extrapolated and reformed by Mardukite Priest-Magicians and the Order of Nabu.

103 See the transliterations available throughout the

preservation of this Babylonian literary tradition on clay tablets rested with the *Order of Nabu*, a secret force that sought to shape the history and future legacy of Babylon in dedication to Marduk. Seeing the popularity of the mystical traditions of Enki to this day, the familiarity with the Marduk-versus-Tiamat archetype, the rising interest in the Babylonian systems and Anunnaki in addition to the Freemason and Illuminati attentions originating with this sect. . . – it is the current author's opinion that the efforts of the *Order of Nabu* proved successful.

Necronomicon Anunnaki Bible edited by Joshua Free.

7. MARDUKITE MONOTHEISM: THE STAR RELIGION OF BABYLON

"Marduk's rise to supremacy did not end polytheism – the religious belief in many gods. On the contrary, his supremacy required continued polytheism, for to be supreme to other gods, the existence of other gods was necessary. He was satisfied to let them be, as long as their prerogatives were subject to his control; but what Marduk expected was that they come and stay with him in his envisaged Babylon – prisoners in golden cages, one may say."

~ Zecharia Sitchin
Earth Chronicles: End of Days, 2007

The appearance of Marduk's "*Star Religion*" sought to 'occult' and conceal the previously laden Sumerian religious designations of the *Elder Gods*. Since it was not systematic, the Sumerian[104] traditions could be easily overlapped with the first clearly defined *systemology*

---

104 See Mardukite *Liber 50*, released to the public as *Sumerian Religion* by Joshua Free.

78

that later serves as an archetype for the planet.[105]
The system integrated into human consciousness was not at first the 'monotheism' that
scholars would recognize by today's *Enlilite*
standards concerning *Jehovah* or the Christian
'God'.[106] Although historians liken this stellar
cult to a true 'monotheistic' standard, the tradition is more correctly termed: *monolatrism*. This
was a confus-ing concept to some, as even the
Assyrians were completely *pantheistic*, exalting
Assur (Marduk), but also venerating and working with many other 'personal' deities.

Babylon became the 'seat of the gods', but by
Mardukite standards, this was to be realized
differently than either *monotheism* or *polythe-*

---

105 Exported forms of this stellar cult also include
Hermetics and Atenism (Egyptian Akhenaton),
Zoroastrianism and Mithraism (Persia); integrated
into the Semitic-Judeo system by Assyrians (and
Akkadians).

106 Hebrew – *El* (Enlil), *Ia-Yahweh* (Enki); early
Christianity separated by Yahwist versus Elohist
sects. Later Christian authorities likened the ancient
myths to 'One God surrounded by lesser angels' but
this still does not adequately explain the
manifestation of the One God on earth as also the all-
present all-knowing all-powerful Divine Source
which is not supposed to be individually manifest
All-as-One. Thus, the existence of Gnosticism,
Elohist Christianity and Mardukite interpretations.

ism. The program became as follows – there are many *gods* but the way is through *One*, idealized in the Babylonian tradition as Marduk and his consort Sarpanit via the 'holy' reception-ists, Nabu[107] and Teshmet.[108] The work done to usurp the ancient *Fifty Names*[109] for Marduk also illuminates the idea of "many *gods* as *One*" or the "*One* manifests with many *faces*," but with the central figure on earth always returning to Marduk as *divine representative*. The system of myth and magic born in Babylon is dedicated to "Marduk's Divine World Order" often illustrated through the first mystical 'kabbalah' system: *10 gates*, *2 doors* and *7 levels* – just like the design for Mardukite ziggurat E.TEMEN. AN.KI – The Temple of Heaven and Earth.[110]

The Mardukite Babylonian Religion[111] is sugge-

---

107 Nabu becomes teacher, speaker, divine secretary of Mardukite Babylon.

108 Teshmet (also Tasmit) is consort to Nabu, the *listener of prayers*.

109 From the *Enuma Elis*, found as the Mardukite Tablet-F Series in the *Necronomicon Anunnaki Bible* edited by Joshua Free.

110 "*Babilu System*" (or *Babili*) – see Mardukite Tablet-B Series in the *Necronomicon Anunnaki Bible* and the follow up material, Mardukite *Liber 50*, released to the public as *Sumerian Religion* by Joshua Free.

111 Now called *Systemology* by the modern Mardukite movement.

stive in many ways of *animism*, the belief that everything possesses an innate or inherent 'spirit' or *Divine Spark* that connects it to 'eternity' or the *All-as-One* (*Divine Source*). By 'everything', we mean the fragmentation of existence that includes any all 'distinct' or 'programmed' vibrational currents – even personalities, personas or identities. From cuneiform tablets we can classify these two aspects as *utukku* (the *Divine Spark* or spiritual essence) and *edimmu* (the identity program of the body).[112] The evolution of the religio-magical systems theories among men can be catalogued as follows:

Sumeria	*unity, celestial-cosmic*
Babylonia	*hierarchy, temple-religions*
Egyptian	*names, magical-mysticism*

Sumeria	*petition to the Most High*
Babylonia	*petition to a pantheon*
Egyptian	*petition to hierarchy of spirits*

Although the Nabu-scribes forged the *Enuma Elis*[113] – a kind of *Epic of Creation* – the purp-

---

112 In the related Egyptian tradition, these aspects are equated to the *ka* (life-force) and *ba* (personality) of an individual being.

113 Discussed later, but a full transliteration is available as the Mardukite Tablet-N Series in the

ose was to bestow Marduk with the *Tablets of Destiny*, enabling him control of World Order. The true beliefs toward cosmogenesis, however, are actually *monistic*. This means that the *Divine Source* represents a single unifying principle or 'element' (referred to in some materials as the *All-as-One*) defining one existence or truth. The perceptions of the variations (*fragmentations*) experienced in the duality of the realm of form are defined, as we have described elsewhere, by the *words* and *language* provided by the perceived authorities. This philosophy and practice of *Hermetic mysticism* is, therefore, not 'invented' by the later classical world, but actually imported.[114]

Necronomicon Anunnaki Bible edited by Joshua Free.
114 In this instance, it moves from Mesopotamia
   through Arabia to Egypt and upward to Greece.

MARDUKITE

8. MESOPOTAMIAN MYTHOLOGY: MARDUK & THE ANUNNAKI

"Like Napolean, who decided he did not need to be crowned according to the rules and crowned himself without further ado, so the Assyrian priests gave the honor to Ashur simply by taking the old Babylonian tablets and recopying them, substituting the name of their own god for that of Marduk. The work was not very carefully done, and in some places the name of Marduk still creeps in. . ."

~ Edward Chiera
They Wrote on Clay, c. 1930

The functional purpose of the cuneiform tablets, in conjunction with the implementation of a social system, surrounded one thing: *religious myths*. The terminology being used concerning the Mesopotamian 'mythos' is not to denote the modern misconception of the word to mean 'fiction' at all. The true meaning of the *mythos* or *mythoi* of human history concerns the *systemology* of human consciousness regarding reality. Thus, the mythology originally was little more than the documentation of history and the deeds of gods, demigods and kings. The central emphasis on these characters is what, in essence, *creates* a mythology – a social paradigm for a large group of people to experience reality. It didn't take long for this methodology to be *covertly manipulated* for the political integrity of the *Babylonian Empire*.

Throughout recorded history, human interaction with the *gods* has been best documented at a particular natural or unnatural terrain – *mountains*. Where the mountains were not accessible, the *gods* in conjunction with the *human workers* constructed 'artificial mountains' or *pyramids*.[115] In the Sumerian language, the word for mountain is *kur*, which also corresponds to the name of the primordial dragon of the universe in pre-Babylon-ian mythology.[116] The first figures to confront[117] this dragon in the Sumerian versions are Enlil, Ninurta and even Inanna-Ishtar, but given that he was busied in Eridu during the development of Sumer, Mar-

---

115 In Mesopotamia they are stepped, like some found in Egypt, and they are called 'ziggurats' (Akkadian – *ziqqurat*; root, *zaqaru*, meaning 'built on a mound').

116 In various places throughout the methodology of the *Anunnaki gods*, at some juncture the 'universe', the 'planet earth' and the 'blood of men' is all termed *dragon*.

117 Archetype – *king of the mountain*.

duk's name is found nowhere on these original tablets.

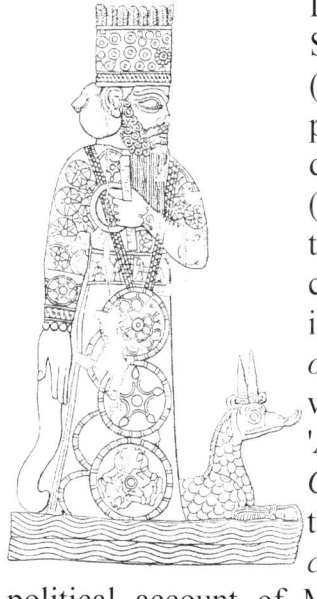

During the ancient Sumerian age, Marduk (*Asarluli*) is the first priest (magician) of Eridu at the temple of Enki (*Ea*), corresponding to the Mesopotamian cult center of antediluvian origins later called *Temple of Poseidon* by the Greek writers concerning an '*Atlantis*'. The *Epic of Creation*[118] brought from this era is not meant to be *cosmogenetic*;[119] instead a political account of Marduk slaying the serpent[120] in the tradition of the pre-Babylonian accounts of *kur*. In doing so, Marduk becomes

118 Called the *Enuma Elis*, given in the *Necronomicon Anunnaki Bible* edited by Joshua Free.

119 Though the epic is set in a time before earth or men and does describe the formation of them both out of the 'created universe', showing the fragmentation of the *All-as-One* into parts. The epic illustrates that as already fragmented beings, the *Anunna* knew of this true-nature of reality and used it to their advantage.

120 Representative of the 'overcoming of chaos' in the universe, meaning: universal or world order.

the self-proclaimed *King of the Anunnaki*,
although the tablet renderings themselves
explain that the title was bestowed upon him as
a reward for the dragon-slaying feat. In doing
this, even if only symbolically and in consciousness, the Mardukite forces are given *Divine
Right* to exercise the powers of the *Anunnaki* on
Earth – thus beginning the Babylonian legacy to
occult Sumerian religion in Mesopotamia.

The *Enuma Elis* forms the cornerstone for the
Mardukite usurpation of the Sumerian hierarchy. The work also illustrates a distinction
between the era and generations who existed
prior to the formation of the priesthood[121] and
the Elder Gods or *Anunna*, who were acknowledged within the Babylonian pantheon under
Marduk.[122] In Eridu, Marduk is actually not
attributed among the *Anunnaki gods* by Sumerian standards and was not listed among the
original hierarchy.[123] As a religio-political 'docu-

---

121 Called the *Ancient Ones* and led by the primordial
   dragon, named *Tiamat* by the Babylonian accounts.
122 Which included many *Enlilite* figures, such as
   Nanna, Inanna-Ishtar, Shammash and Nergal.
123 In fact, Marduk is actually listed as a primary leader
   of the Igigi-Watchers, setting a status quo in Eridu
   and then Babylon, concerning the intermarriage with
   humans. For this 'indiscretion' by Enlilite standards
   he was denied his *Divine Right*, but his argument

ment', the *creation cycle*[124] is similar to the "Donation of Constantine"[125] that was responsible for the Church attaining *Divine Right* and the worldly means to execute it. Following a dramatically unsuccessful campaign much earlier in Sumerian history,[126] the *Enuma Elis* program is officially installed c. 2150 B.C. by the Mardukite Nabu-Priests.

The origins of the *Dragon of Babylon* are obscure and involve a part of the *Anunnaki* lineage that was not so well preserved – most likely for political reasons. Marduk, himself, has two brothers, both by Enki but not necessarily Ninki:[127] Ningizida, also given as *Ningishzidda* or *Ni(n)rah* and *Ninazu* or *Tis(h)pak*. The Babylonian accounts reveal that the dragon really did exist, that it first belonged to Tispak, later owned by Marduk (as often

---

remained that it was never going to be given to him anyway and that his chosen consort, Sarpanit, was actually of royal blood by Enki (being the descendent of Adapa).

124 Which historians and biblical scholars also note to be the basis origins of the Judeo-Christian *Genesis*.

125 Another famous political 'forgery' used to gain worldly power.

126 Resulting in the 'Tower of Babel' incident – see also Mardukite *Liber 50*, released to the public as *Sumerian Religion* by Joshua Free.

127 The name given for the mother of Marduk.

shown in popular depictions) and eventually came to be in the care of Nabu. The render-ing that was left by Nabuchadnezzar near the *Ishtar Gate* can still be seen.

The name of the dragon is *Sirius* or *Sirrus*[128] and should not be confused with the *usumgal*, or 'Great Serpent' used to represent the universe. In the African Congo, the description of the beast matches a thought-to-be extinct *sauropod* called the *mokele-mbembe* by indigenous tribes who have claimed to have killed one. This would effectively connect dragon-lore with din-

---

128 Also given as *sirush* and *sirrush* – a name derived from the Akkadian word *mushussu* or *mushhushshu*, meaning 'furious serpent'. The Univeristy of Pennsylvania catalogues list *mus-hus* as "monster."

osaurs[129] and possibly even the distant nomenclature of the phonetics – *sa-ru-us* to *saurus*.
Mastery of a dragon has been associated with
godhood since the early renderings concerning
the slaying of *kur* by early leaders of the
Anunnaki gods.[130] The overt possession of a live
dragon as both a *royal pet* and *icon* of the holy
city led to securing the worldly 'seat of god' in
Babylon as an archetypal image guaranteed by
the consciousness of the masses.

---

129 Where dragon-lore has been found to be universal,
   contemporary knowledge (evidence) of dinosaurs has
   only been in public awareness for the last 200 years.
130 Evidence of this remains in Judeo-Christian lore,
   however, the *One God* was eventually seen as 'too
   great' to be concerned with mortal battle and so the
   'dragon-slaying' motif was passed on to 'ambassadors'
   of God, first St. Michael (the archangel closely
   associated with Marduk) and then St. George.

MARDUKITE

9. BASE-60: MEASURING SPACE-TIME

"The Old Babylonian period was a time of great advancement for the development of what would be called the 'sciences'. Yet it was one 'science' in particular that characterized the Babylonians' world view – astrology. By the beginning of the first millennium B.C., the Babylonians had developed skywatching skills and utilized them in the making of a calendar and a system of mathematics, based on the sexagesimal system, to track and simulate the motion of the Sun and Moon."

J. P. McEvoy (1999)
Eclipse – Science & History

The ancient Sumerians understood the connection between cycles, time and mathematics. In addition to the pragmatic use of the wheel or circle, they also developed the initial calculations of the circle to be 360 degrees. Their use of base-60 '*sexagesimal*' math[131] in the systematic

---

131 Detailed explanation appears in the 'Mesopotamian Numerology' appendix of Mardukite *Liber 50*, released to the public as *Sumerian Religion* (also known as *Gates of the Necronomicon*) by Joshua

measurement of time has carried with humanity to this day.[132] The annual year[133] was originally only divided into three seasons: beginning, middle and end.[134]

A year in *Babylonia* was separated into a cycle of 12 periods of 30 degrees or days. These periods, equated to the 'moon', were called '*moonths*' or more appropriately 'months'. Of course, the sky-wise priests were aware of the actual appearance of 13 lunar cycles in a year, so an additional shortened month was acknowledged to make the cycle fit.[135] In most cases, a 'new moon' meant a 'new month' and so the days counted in a month are the days counted in the progression of a moon – though naturally the disparities between lunar and solar time had to be accounted for, and with time the 'Chaldeans'[136] had perfected it.

Free.

132 Where hours are made up of 60 minutes containing 60 seconds each.

133 Annual Year – *sat-ti.*

134 Beginning, "*res sat-ti*"; Middle, "*misil sat-ti*"; and End, "*kit sat-ti.*"

135 Even by today's standards the system requires leap-years and does not account for the ever-changing position of celestial bodies as they move steadily towards or away from one another.

136 *Chaldeans* – A Greek classification of the Nabu priesthood during the *Babylonian Renaissance* and

The annual cycle was marked distinctly by two primary religious festivals – the spring festival of Akitu[137] and the winter festival of Zagmuk.[138] Both appear to be represented or distinguished by the symbol of '*divine marriage*', later meaning the relationship between the ruling king and his lands. Originally, however, the more popular *fertility* interpretation of these festivals, particularly in the spring, were based on *land renewal* and with the development and spread of these tradition, *Akitu* became known as *Ostara* – the pagan *Easter* – in dedication to Ishtar (Inanna).

---

reformation period (c. 700 B.C.) during which the historical (mythic) and astronomical tablet documents were of considerable interest. The term 'Chaldean' is a Greek interpretation of what otherwise is not wholly separate from the continued legacy of *Babylonia*. However, there is reason to believe that this later Babylonian group had encounters and exchanges with the *Druids*, whereby the Celts had originally inherited additional cabalistic and 'Semitic' lore from Babylon, which also served their own secret society of lore-masters, classified as the *Khalde* or *Kuldee*, of a similar phonetics.

137 Also given as *A-ki-ti* (meaning: *on earth, life*) observed as the Spring Equinox, also marking the Mesopotamian *New Year* and first month of *Nisan*.

138 The pagan Christmas or Yule observed as the Winter Solstice as a time when the "*God-King*" returns or is reborn, usually reflective among European traditions of the Sun's absence and then return, wholly agricultural in nature.

Not too surprisingly, the pre-Christian account incorporated into the symbolism of the later Judeo-based traditions also includes the proverbial theme of *resurrection* – in our case: the infamous story of Ishtar's '*descent*' into the '*Underworld*', where she is perceived of as 'dead' for *three days*.

Given the way modern calendars are oriented, the start of each ancient month would be considered near the 'middle' of current months[139] – much like the seasonal observations.[140] Although the festivals in ancient times were oriented to the naturally occurring *solstices* and *equinoxes*, it was often customary to observe them ceremonially during the closest full moon.[141] All of this gave way to a generally 'fluid' incorporation of time into society that is varied in its interpretations among modern sch-

---

139 Just as we might expect of the astrological or 'zodiac' months.

140 Both the Spring and Autumn Equionx and the Summer and Winter Solstice are all generally 'observed' on the 21st of the respective months: March, September, June and December. In contemporary calendars these might also be referred to as "First day of. . ." the appropriate season.

141 But this certainly was not a rule, just as the fluidity of time in general, and the ancient astronomical tablets are, of all of them, the most difficult to interpret with certainty by modern historians.

olars.

The ancients made use of 'water-clocks' at night and 'sun-clocks' during the day. But more important to the survival of an agricultural society then gauging the minutes of a day for a 'time-punch' was the tracking of the annual cycle for planting and harvesting.

Quite different than what the remainder of the *Western World* has familiarity with, the seasonal cycles in the deserts of *Babylonia* are unique.

We have a recognizable summer in June, July and August where there is not rain and nothing grows – as we might expect – but then the region is plunged right into its rainy season in Sept-ember, and farmers must be ready to plant their barley by October with a harvest necessary before the summer sun returns.

A different system of observation was used to calculate and measure '*divine time*'[142] in relation

---

142 Technically "*Celestial Time*" – That which related to the zodiacal wheel of the 'Celestial Sphere' – each measured as 30 degrees of the circumference of the 'Sphere', giving rise to 12 'zodiacal' divisions.
"*Divine Time*" is calculated by the *shar* and is 3,600 years according to most interpretations.

to '*earth time*'.[143] This gave rise to what contemporaries call an '*age*' – such as the current '*age*' of Pisces and the forthcoming '*age*' of Aquarius. Apart from the garbled nonsense of today's *horoscopes*, the observation of *zodiacal* ages and alignments during the year are very real events. For whatever credibility the modern mind might wish to give the ancient *astrologie omen* tablets,[144] the ability to perfectly chart time over long periods by using verifiable astronomical events, that we can even rely on today as investigators into this ancient culture, is quite impressive by any standards.

We can establish the chronological procession of the ages, but not necessarily a definition of when they have absolute turning points. They are measured in 2,160 year periods (72 x 30), connected to their 'domain' of visibility in the 'Celestial Sphere'.[145] The progression is visible

---

143 Defined by the relationship between the Earth and the Sun and Moon.

144 Not so much 'predictions' as they are 'general advisement', usually drawn up for Kings by their priests. The time-keeping efforts are impressive, however the *omens* themselves are generally of the nature of: 'beware of ladders on such-and-such a day, because if you fall off of one you will get hurt.' (well, hm...)

145 An observable ring of specific constellations relative to earth that became known as the *zodiac*.

in the stars but the clear boundary line that defines each is in many ways obscure. For example, when specifically does the current age enter 'Aquarius'? Counting backward, the *Mardukite* school of thought might have suggestive input to apply.[146]

Following earlier thwarted attempts to solidify global rulership, the real *Babylonian Reformation* by the *Anunnaki god* Marduk, with the aid of Nabu, occurred as a result of the '*Age of Aries*' having arrived and 'promised power' not being 'passed' to him. This would have to be circa 2150 B.C., when the movement became notably public.

How long prior to this, pointing to the turn of the '*Age of Aries*', would they have waited? If it were only *ten years*, then the Piscean Age *really would* have been marked by the birth of Jesus Christ – *exactly* 2,160 years later – notoriously represented by the *fishes*. Other 'scholarly' dates for the start of the Age of Aries include 2200,[147]

---

146 The 'Chaldeans' noted the discovery of the 'Saros' (*sar* meaning *cycle* or *recursive*), a cyclic period by which eclipses can be observed. More details on this are given as the *Book of Eclipses & The Astrologie* (Tablet E-Series) found within the *Necronomicon Anunnaki Bible* edited by Joshua Free.

147 Zecharia Sitchin – c. 2200 B.C. (based on the

2150,[148] 2000 and 1875 B.C.[149] Based on these figures, this 'era' of reportedly 'new consciousness' could be in effect now, later in this century, in the year 2150 or even closer to 2600.[150] Time, as we have found no different today then yesterday, is indeed *entirely* relative.

ANNUAL YEAR
[Sumerian – Akkadian]
1. Nisannu – Nisan (*spring equinox*)
2. Airu – Iyyar
3. Simanu – Siwan
4. Du'uzu – Tammuz
5. Abu – Ab
6. Ululu – Elul
7. Tishritu – Tisri (*autumn equinox*)
8. Arahsamna – Marchesvan
9. Kislimu – Kislev
10. Tebitu – Tebet
11. Shabatu – Sebat
12. Addau – Adar
13. "Second Adar" (*extra month*)

---

alignment at Stonehenge)
148 Neil Mann – c. 2150 B.C. (based on the general division of 30 degrees)
149 Shephard Simpson – c. 1875 B.C. (based on the physical constellation boundary)
150 Based on the location of the physical constellation, not simply the divisions of 30 degrees.

ZODIAC NAMES

1. Ku-mal (Aries)
2. Gu-an-na (Taurus)
3. Mash-tab-ba (Gemini)
4. Dub (Cancer)
5. Ur-gula (Leo)
6. Ab-sin (Virgo)
7. Zi-bi-an-na (Libra)
8. Gir-tab (Scorpio)
9. Pa-bil (Sagittarius)
10. Su-hur-mash (Capricorn)
11. Gu (Aquarius)
12. Sim-mah (Pisces)

10. BABYLONIAN MAGIC: THE ART OF PRIESTS

"Systematic traditions, 'hermetically sealed' within themselves, rose from the Semitic grimoire-styled ceremonial magick, not surprisingly influenced by 'Egypto-Babylonian' forms of ritual magick (first the domain of Enki but later passed into the possession of Marduk and his scribe-son Nabu). The priest-magicians of Babylon would not actually have personally used a grimoire-like magick themselves, as this not their way. At best, they would invoke the powers of the Anunnaki with incantations in the name of Marduk – but this manner of using the 'secret names' as properties of Marduk, or any other demigod, was a much more recent addition to the system. . ."

~ Joshua Free
Mardukite Liber R, 2010

In the midst of a relative '*New Age movement*' led by '*esotericists*' toward the uncovering of the pragmatic and ritualistic elements of pagan and occult methodologies, it should seem that we would have little trouble with this in Mesopotamia – being the origins of these later *systems*. Without some assistance, however, this is not necessarily as simply done as pouring through a *kabbalastic grimoire* written by some *medieval sorcerer*. While there was surely no shortage of 'superstitions' among the masses, such as the carrying of 'amulets' among commoners – certainly, this type of folk tradition does not constitute a real *system* of magic. For this, a *seeker* will have to dig a little harder in the desert sands.

During the era of the first *ziggurat* temples – the *Anunnaki* age – all of the magic constituted the 'spiritual assistance' that was governed by the state, ruled by priest-kings and other temple attendants. The 'mystics' of *Babylonia* were all employed by the temples and scribe-houses, though there were undoubtedly those who confined themselves to their arts in the *outlands*, beyond the awareness of the societal realm. The peasant class, however, did not practice much by way of 'magic' (as classified by anthropologists) outside of their own personal religious devotions, which in itself was mostly restricted to *hymns* and *prayers* learned from the temples.[151] These personal devotions

---

151 The modern *Mardukite* pursuits into said *hymns*, *prayers* and other 'invocations' became the main tenet

were also completely inclination-based, as there does not appear to be any prescribed devotional method or temple attendance *required* of a Babylonian citizen, nor even participation in national festivals.

Tablets concerned with the conduct of various ceremonies describe religious artifacts that are not items the average person would have had possession of, initially suggesting that, indeed, any of the *magic* from this period was restricted to the priests. The use of a temple, for one, appears key. Access to the '*incantation-pray-ers*'[152] of the priests were also not generally given to just anyone – and you had to be able to read them, or at the very least memorize them.[153] The Altar of Offering set before the

---

of study and development of the *libros*: N, L, G and 9 (which all appear in the *Necronomicon Anunnaki Bible* edited by Joshua Free) in addition to that which appear in the *Mardukite Liber 50* (*Sumerian Religion*) and its original companion, *The Book of Marduk by Nabu* – all released by the Mardukite Truth Seeker Press.

152 General collections of these tablets were seldom kept, with the exception of priest-kings who might house their own personal libraries. An example being the Kuyunjik collection, called *nis kati* (now in the British Museum) which was the private property of the Assyrian king Ashurbanipal.

153 Possibly contributing to the rise of the 'oral tradition'

'*Boat of the Gods*'[154] was also located at the official shrines – although personal altars could surely be constructed by a devotee to appeal to their *god*, this would have come much later during the era of '*figurative mysticism*' because originally, these offerings would have been physically received by a *god* in person, or via their 'priestly secretaries'.

Common religious offerings included food and drink, incense and oil, all the way to lavish jewelry and clothing – which were carried up the *ziggurat* steps of the '*ladder to heaven*' to be placed before the feet of the *god*, or at the very least, at his '*boat*' to be lifted to them. When the appearance of the *gods*, themselves, was not present, it was customary to have an *official* piece of statuary left in there place. This became more and more figurative with the passage of time, and it is easy to see how many of these originating concepts evolved into later *magical* and *religious* practices – which were one and the same at their start.

---

where knowledge is passed from teacher to apprentice unwritten.

154 This imagery also appears in the Egyptian Tradition – a 'Boat of the Gods' carrying seven figures – e.g. the principle *Seven Anunnaki Gods* of the Babylonian 'Younger Generation'.

White was the most common color worn by the priests, although black was also used and was even favored by the temple-priestesses. The attire of the priests and priestesses would include the infamous 'conical hat' that has not only been popularly associated with classical 'wizards', but use of it can be found in the visual and literary depictions of the *gods*, kings and priests of both ancient *Babylonia* and Egypt. Several of these highly valued ceremonial implements used in the temple even appear in the mythic tales of the *gods*.[155] For example, the *shu-gu-ra*, the conical '*starry crown of Anu*' previously described.

Gold and *lapis lazuli* appear to be the two most commonly found elements or materials used as both 'magical ritual aids' and prestigious 'offerings' to the temples, suggesting that the later may have led to the former. Wands, necklaces and bags of loose *lapis* are mentioned often as well as golden rings and 'amulet-plates' marked with specific seals and cuneiform writing.[156]

---

155 The *seven* "decrees" worn by the goddess in *The Descent of Inanna-Ishtar to the Underworld*, described in *Mardukite Liber 50*, as well as the full text of the cycle as the 'Tablet-C Series' in the *Necronomicon Anunnaki Bible* edited by Joshua Free.
156 Practical investigations into this later developed into

The implementation of a practical magical system from the Babylonian ideal is somewhat different than what the contemporary mind, even an '*esoteric*' one, is fundamentally familiar with. As opposed to the later magicians who appear to have had to connive and fool the hierarchies of spirits into assisting them, sometimes threatening them and even in fear of some retroactive revenge – the original magical system used by the priests of *Babylonia* was rooted in the deep personal relationship – running as deep as *blood* – that the Sumerian priest-kings and Nabu priest-scribes maintained with the sources of not only their religious power, but the basis of the entire system of civilization that allowed the progression of the human species into today. All of this, according to tradition, resided in the influence of the *Anunnaki gods* – and the priest-kings and scribes were installed to be sure no one forgot this.

---

a modern standard used by the *Mardukites* illustrating sigil-seals and cuneiform signatures of the *seven* of the "Younger Generation" as well as the *Supernal Trilogy* – making ten sets in total. These were originally integrated into *Liber GG* (in 2009) as found in the *Necronomicon Anunnaki Bible*. They were later reprinted in *Liber 50* and the *Book of Marduk by Nabu*.

11. STARFIRE – CEREMONIES TO THE ANUNNAKI

"True indeed, there was a supreme name which possessed the power of commanding the gods and extracting from them a perfect obedience, but that name remained the inviolable secret of Enki. In exceptional cases the priest besought Enki, through the mediator Marduk, to pronounce the solemn word in order to reestablish order in the world and restrain the powers of the Abyss. But the priest did not know that name, and could not in consequence introduce it into his formulae. . . he could not obtain or make use of it, he only requested the god who knew it to employ it, without endeavoring to penetrate the terrible secret himself."

~ M. Lenormant
Chaldean Magic & Sorcery (1874)

Compared to a later world of folk traditions – where love potions run rampant and the possession of wealth is as a matter of spinning around seven times while whistling and throwing feathers to the north winds – the original stoic and sacred rites of magic are rooted in a tradition based on a direct relationship with '*sky gods*' that later become assimilated second- (or third-) hand by cultures all over the globe. The hierarchy of the *Anunnaki gods* among themselves and in relation to worldly affairs of humans gave rise to a mystical concept of '*spiritual pantheons*'. These pantheons were later catalogued by *kabbalistic magicians* in their attempts to uncover the 'secret of the ages', or more specifically, the secret '*magical word*' to gain authority with the *forces* of the *cosmos*.

Efforts made by modern interpreters[157] of the ancient mystical tablets of *Babylonia* has resulted in a formatted ritual-text outline that appears consistent with those found among the collections in museums and archives. In terms of modern revival for a practitioner or group,[158] the ancient ideology laid out thus far in our present volume, particularly in relation to the

---

157 The division of the Mardukite Ministries organization dedicated to experimental research and development of the Mesopotamian Anunnaki revival paradigm, specific to *Babylonia*, known as the *Mardukite Chamberlains*.

158 Such as we see common in the 'New Age' in the forms of *neodruidism*, *wicca* and other 'occult' or 'pagan' revivals based in a particular cultural system or mystical paradigm.

Anunnaki and *Babylonian Magic*, should be kept in mind.[159] Following both the offerings of 'quantum psychology' and the 'practical mystic', the energetic self does not necessarily distinguish a reality barrier between what it encounters as experience in the more relatively familiar 'day-to-day' realm from what is possible in properly executed ritual drama. In ancient times, the priests reinforced this in society through the dramatic reenactments of the ancient myths, thereby making for a social consciousness that more easily allowed this *magic* to become *reality*. All of it, of course, being a matter of *perspective*.

The Babylonian Religio-Magic System was developed by the ancient *Mardukites* as a means of sealing the power of the older generation of *gods* under Marduk, with him holding 'kingship' over the younger generation that served the devotional needs of post-Sumerian *Babylonia*. Thus, cosmic power was accessed *through him* and worldly power was dispatched *by him*. And,

---

159 Symbolism and representation appears key among mystical revival traditions. For example, in the absence of access to the shrines of Babylon and physical ziggurat temples, modern practitioners often use 'creative visualization' or other more *esoteric* methods of 'astral travel' to connect with the same 'energetic forces'.

so long as they could be honored within the confines of the prescribed system, figures such as Inanna-Ishtar, Nergal, Nanna and Shammash-Samas all appear within the younger pantheon[160] observed by the *Mardukites* even though they are *not* descendents of Enki.[161] Doing so increased the appeal and acceptance of the *system* to the Sumerians at large and the desired shift toward a *Mardukite* interpretation of the image of these *gods*, their governing domains and their position in the universal hierarchy – all sealed within human consciousness. In Babylon, the '*sealing*' of this *system* became interpreted literally as the *Gates of the Gods*.[162]

A modern revival 'Gatekeeping' or 'Gatewalk-

---

160 Composed of seven – Nanna-Sin, Nabu, Inanna-Ishtar, Shammash-Samas, Nergal, Marduk and Ninurta. From this list, only Marduk and Nabu are '*Priests of Eridu*', meaning 'sons' of Enki.

161 Often referred to in the incantations as "*Our Father*," speaking from the perspective of either Marduk or Nabu. Depending on the use, this is sometimes equated to Anu instead, the distant "Heavenly Father."

162 *Babu* – 'gate' and *Ilu* or *Ili* – as 'gods' or possibly an obscure reference to the 'Divine Source' which was later religiously equated with Anu, who governed 'heaven' (see *Mardukite Liber 50*, released as *Sumerian Religion* or *Gates of the Necronomicon*).

ing'[163] tradition can be derived from the ancient literature that describes a time when the priests and magicians of the people were working alongside the *Anunnaki gods* in the establishment and preservation of these *gates* and *shrines*. Following in the pious footsteps of the priests of *Babylonia*, whether a modern *seeker* or revivalist *practitioner* has been truly *self-honestly* dedicated to the *system* or not, the often primordial power of these currents, to be useful – or channeled directly – must be first respected, and thus the path requires one to cumulatively build this authority while working with the pantheon, following the way of the ancient 'devotional' kings, priests and scribes. The *magic*, then, comes directly from the *working* relationship the individual (priest or magician) maintains with the "powers" believed to control the domains desired to be influenced.[164]

According to the *Mardukite Tablet-B Series*[165]

---

163 As it has been called among a faction of modern 'occultists' since the 1970's.

164 Paragraph based on the article, *First Steps Toward Gatekeeping* (for *Mardukite Liber GG*) by Joshua Free.

165 Relayed in the *Necronomicon Anunnaki Bible* edited by Joshua Free, and again quoted in the "Ceremonial Formulae" appendix of *Mardukite Liber 50*

concerning effective ritual revival:

"The priest is always to observe the pious ways, and the Rites of Offering at the Altar of Sacrifice. This is traditional performed by intoning prayers [incantations] from the tablets in conjunction with the offering of incense, grain [bread], honey [with butter] and libations of buttermilk (and in some cases, wine). Sacred or "holy" oil [and water] make an appearance in virtually all ancient Babylonian rites – the water and oil frequently placed in bowls before icons [of deities] in temples, in addition to offerings of alabaster, gold and lapis lazuli."

Where the temple is not accessible, '*magic carpets*' and '*statuary*'[166] can be set out to consecrate an area for the purposes of *priestly magic*. As has continued with the tradition to present-day, the most common form of sacred space (outside of the temple) is in the form of a *mandala* or 'sacred circle'. Being both traditional and agricultural, the boundary of the circle was marked by the consecrated "*flour of*

(*Sumerian Religion*).

166 Some ritual texts refer to an '*image of your god and goddess*' where others refer to an arranged line of '*seven winged figures*' indicative of the *seven-Anunnaki* of the 'Younger Generation'.

Nisaba"[167] in the same way modern '*esotericists*' might draw theirs in chalk, etc.

As advice to the priest or magician, the *Mardukite Tablet-Q Series*[168] offers this step:

"*Make your invocation to Marduk and Sarpanit. Then call in [invoke] the Supernal Trinity – Anu, Enlil and Enki, followed by a conjuration [consecration] of the Fire and the Four Beacons [lamps] of the Watchtowers [cardinal directions]. Perform the 'Incantation of Eridu' and call forth the presence of your personal sedu [guardian watcher spirit].*"

The *sedu* is the origins of the Assyrian concept that later became relayed as a "guardian angel." According to Babylonian beliefs, every person had one.[169] The incorporation of this belief in the midst of the *Anunnaki* tradition is something of a mystery unless it is directly a part of the persons individual 'astral' core or 'spirit'. Other-

---

167 Which later became the *Flour of Nabu*, with the evolution of the Babylonian mythos.

168 Relayed in *Mardukite Liber 9*, reprinted in both the *Necronomicon Anunnaki Bible* and *Novem Portis – Necronomicon Revelations* (revised *Nine Gates*).

169 Although this belief may not have been shared by all since found in the lines of some incantations are requests to "acquire" a *sedu* and a *lamassu*.

wise, it is suggestive of an inter-dimensional nature to the *Igigi-Watchers* that were subordinate to the *Anunnaki* pantheon, and that they somehow tracked along with a person – unnoticed – during the course of their life. The reason it is mysterious for these benevolent spirits to be of this nature is because the *malignant* forces later equated as 'demonic spirits' were not so 'invisible', and were instead the actual pestilence and biological warfare employed by the *Anunnaki gods* (and later *demigods* and kings).

Given that most of the catalogued *taboo*-sins[170] were meant to keep the people clean and free of infections and disease, and the laws were meant to keep people civil without having to murder or eat one another, it seems clear (in light of the true nature of the *Anunnaki* and the technologies employed as *spirituality*) that the deeper purposes behind religious traditions may indeed hide truly 'occult' secrets. Nonetheless, strict personal cleanliness was required among priests, not only in their conductance of ceremony, but in their everyday walking lives as well. Keeping hair trimmed, or even shaved,

---

170 Explored in the "Tablet-H Series" of *Mardukite Liber 9* (contained in the *Necronomicon Anunnaki Bible* and *Novem Portis*).

was also a part of daily ritual,[171] and even the original use of eye makeup, once thought to be purely decorative, appears to have had some evolutionary advantages in the desert.[172]

While tablet transliterations have indeed been found for these *prayers* and *invocations*,[173] even a casual study of them will reveal that they are simply *personal appeals* – they have not yet taken on the more recent incorporation of '*secret formulas*' or '*divine names*' in magical work. The key elements involve speaking the names of the deities being invoked, sometimes several of their 'names' or mythic 'titles', and also the presentation (or supplication) of the priest before this entity.[174] All of the spoken words involved are really, then, quite direct. *Who are you? Who are you calling? What is the message?* – Just like dealing with a *divine secretary*, and yes, the Babylonians installed

---

171 Such aided in thwarting personal insect infestations.

172 Using black 'eye-shadow', particularly below the eyes (as seen by today's athletes), assists in reducing the sun-glare received from the open sandy areas.

173 Examined in the Mardukite Chamberlains cycle in the *libros* – N, L, G, 9 and 50.

174 Also involving (traditionally) the recitation of a short parentage – for example, "*I, so-and-so, the son of so-and-so and so-and-so, whose god and goddess is so-and-so and so-and-so. . .*"

Nabu and Teshmet to this very real position!

Keep in mind that the entire effectiveness of the priest's magical work was based on their personal relationship with the *gods* – not simply their ability to discern a *secret number* or precisely memorize an *incantation formula*.[175] Thus, the ritualized *petitions* for assistance appear to be more comparable to requesting help from a *friend* or *authority* – and as such there is a certain measure of *tact*, perhaps common sense, that later became integrated as "occult correspondences." Here – *This one is only home after 5. This one is more content around the smell of roses. Offer to take this one to lunch first. Mondays are NOT this one's day!* Etc. etc.[176]

---

175 These later '*mystical*' beliefs were incorporated more recently (historically speaking) in magical systems, originating in Egypt.

176 Those who made this work their everyday lives in the temples generally knew this type of information, particularly in regards to the singular deity they probably were dealing with regularly. The appearance of 'grimoires', 'spellbooks' and unauthorized 'prayerbooks' among the masses emerged during the evolution of the system by those usually 'outside' the ranks of the tradition and generally not privy to the sanctity involved. In one extension of the Mesopotamian tradition, this can be seen exactly as just described with the evolution of the Semitic

Perhaps the most fundamental 'formula' of the magical system in *Babylonia*, if there is one, goes back to the heart of the *system* born of the scribe-priests and the figures who brought this *system* about – *Nabu* and the appropriation of his father, *Marduk* as the chief director. This is what is alluded to by the *Incantation of Eridu*,[177] whereby a practitioner assumes the representative form of the "*Priest of Eridu*," a title first bestowed upon Marduk by Enki, and then passed to Nabu. The key here is that the priest conducts the incantations (ceremony) as the embodiment of this deity,[178] thereby directing the cosmic order, in essence, *first hand*. In short – the magician *approaches* his deity as himself – *a servant priest* – and petitions to assume the *godform*, whereby he continues the ceremony as a *divine representation* of the *god*[179] – in this

---

Kabbalah, where knowledge and use of it eventually migrated 'outside' the *rabbinical*.

177 Also known as the '*Incantation of the Priest of Eridu*' (Eridu being the shrine-home of Enki) or the '*Incantation of the Deep*', simply referring to yet another name for the abode of Enki.

178 The very origin and semantic meaning of "*invocation*."

179 An almost identical set of principles appear at the heart of Semitic mysicism and the Judeo-Kabbalah. In fact, even in contemporary *Catholicism*, the priest 'assumes the *christform*' to effectively perform religio-alchemical transmutation on the sacramental

present system: Marduk. This is affirmed the priest's first utterance of : "*It is not I, but Marduk, who speaks the incantation.*" And now the *system* is *sealed* and readied for use.

Consider the lines in this conjuration:[180]

> *It is not I, but Marduk, Slayer of Serpents,*
> *Who summons thee.*
> *It is not I, but Enki, Father of the Magicians,*
> *Who calls thee here now.*

An examination of the remaining lines of the '*Incatation of Eridu*' appears here, though the "Mardukite" version is given fully in the *Tablet-Y Series*. As described, the ritual operates as if from the perspective of Nabu (speaking for Marduk). Though variations exist in the opening of several Assyrian "exorcisms," one key tablet[181] relates:

> *The Priest of EA [Enki] am I.*

---

bread and wine, conducted as a representative of Jesus on earth.

180 Adapted from the Mardukite "*Conjuration of the Fire God*" from the Tablet-Y Series of *Liber GG*, contained in the *Necronomicon Anunnaki Bible* edited by Joshua Free.

181 Translated by R.C. Thompson as his "Tablet N" for *Devils and Evil Spirits of Babylonia* (1903).

The priest of Damkina [Ninki] am I.
The messenger [nabu] of Marduk am I.
My spell is the spell of EA [Enki].
My incantation is the incantation of Marduk.
The 'magic circle' of EA [Enki] is in my hand.
The tamarask,[182] in my hand, I hold.

From the modernized *Mardukite* version, the opening lines read:[183]

I am the Priest of Marduk,
Son of Our Father, Enki.
I am the Priest of Eridu,
And the Magician of Babylon.

The Assyrian version continues humbly as follows:

EA [Enki], King of the Deep
See me favorably.
I, the magician, am thy slave.
March thou on my right hand,
Assist me on my left;
Add thy pure spell to mine.
Add thy pure voice to mine.
O god that blesses me, Marduk,

---

182 An obscure crystalline "laser" used by Anu.
183 From Tablet-Y Series in the *Necronomicon Anunnaki Bible* edited by Joshua Free.

Let me be blessed, wherever my path rests.
Thy power, shall god and man proclaim.
And I too, the magician, thy slave.

Returning to a Babylo-Akkadian version,[184] we see a slightly different method used in petitioning the "younger pantheon" to the side of the priest.

I am the Priest of EA [Enki].
I am the Magician of Eridu.
Shammash [Samas] is before me.
Sin [Nanna] is behind me.
Nergal is at my right hand.
Ninurta is at my left hand.

And to this, the *Mardukite* version appends:

Anu, above me, King of Heaven.
Enki, below me, King of the Deep.
The power [blood] of Marduk is within me.
It is not I, but Marduk, who performs the
    incantation.

With this, the priest has mystically shed the 'mortal spark' of his nature, even if for a moment, to experience the *transcendental mag-*

_____

184 Transliterated by E.A. Budge for his *Babylonian Life & History* (1883).

ic that is to be clad in *godhood*. Rising on the planes of perceptual awareness – as a *god*, speaking on behalf of the *chief* of the pantheon – the priest-magician is now able to influence worldly affairs in the *original* and most direct magical means known on the planet – a direct interface with the *gods* as one of their own.

TABLET OF UNION[185]

All life is precious in the fact that it lives.
Life *is* – existing against all odds,
and Life grows and develops following a
course.

Love is Will and Love creates emotions.
Love is everything.

God the Supreme Being is that which represents
True Pure All-Powerful Love;
the Light that binds the Universe
in Creation & Destruction.
God is the conscience in all Life.
When you put the Love & Light that is God

---

185 Debuting in a Mardukite literary release entitled,
Marduk & The Anunnaki (Spring 2009) prior to
production of the current literary cycle for the
Mardukite Truth Seeker Press. It made a widespread
public appearance in the *Liber N* materials that have
now reached thousands, originally catalogued in the
Book of Last Days or "Tablet-R Series"
(*Necronomicon Anunnaki Bible*). It has frequently
appeared in the appendices of many *Mardukite*
releases, both public and private. The modern
Chamberlain *author-transliterator* first connected
with this now famous piece has been identified only
as *Merodach*.

into something it becomes Eternal.

The Devil is a name for the path that leads one
to harm another and themselves,
the belief that one can live without Love.

You cannot exist without Love.

All Life is One in Equality.
Love is even within Evil for it to exist,
as Love in Evil creates the Demons
of Jealousy, Misery, Greed, Pain and Grief.

In and of the Love of God,
Man & Woman can manifest creations of Love.
The power to create is in Love.
The power to destroy is in Love.

To live for yourself alone outside Love
is unity with Greed.

As the Love of God is in all Life,
the Natural State of All Life
is to Love All Life.

Would you like to know more???

Enter the Realm of the

**MARDUKITE
CHAMBERLAINS**

NECRONOMICON ANUNNAKI BIBLE
Edited by Joshua Free

The Necronomicon – a masterpiece of Mesopotamian Magick, Mysticism and primordial spirituality!

A Complete Necronomicon!

This definitive edition contains the complete Year 1 tablet cycle from the "Mardukite Chamberlains" including Liber N – ***Necronomicon***, Liber LL – *Liturgy & Lore*, Liber GG – *Gatekeepers Grimoire* and the coveted Liber 9. These are the raw underground materials have shaped the existence of man's beliefs and practices for thousands of years – right from the heart of Sumer, Babylon and Egypt! A Mardukite compendium of intensive historical, spiritual and mystical research drawn from very real and researchable tablets... enough to support a very real "*Necronomicon*" Anunnaki revival tradition!

Join hundreds of others who have enjoyed the best of what the next generation has to offer. What has come before is but a shadow to the realizations now capable to all self-honest Truth Seekers! Rediscover the most ancient records of magick and mysticism – the most ancient traditions of Gods and Men lay here waiting to be unveiled!

MARDUKITE

THE BOOK OF ELVEN-FAERIE
by Joshua Free

The original underground masterpiece *comes alive* and in print available to the public for the *first time ever!*

Follow the ancient traditions of Mesopotamia as they evolve into the systems of Western Europe.

Discover how the most arcane practices actually shaped the beliefs of the western world and learn how mystical lineages of modern "folk magic" can be actually traced through the evolution of human civilization on the planet – all the way back to the ancient Anunnaki traditions of Sumerians, Babylonians, Egyptians, etc. and becoming the practices of the Tuatha de Dannan (Tuatha d'Anu) and other Celtic tribes.

Ever popular in the underground, this book includes the complete *Book of Elven-Faerie* discourse with its corresponding "Grimoires" of Elven-Faerie traditions and forest magick, bring a com-plete Elvish Tradition to light for the first time in printed history. This book restores the historical basis of the modern "New Age" movements resulting from one Seeker's pursuits into the origins of the "Druids."

MARDUKITE

SUMERIAN RELIGION
by Joshua Free

The most highly acclaimed materials from the Marduk-ites: an account of the evolution of the Sumerian Tradition into Babylonian (and beyond) such as the modern world has never be-fore had access to.

Developed by the next gen-eration of seekers actively using this revival tradition in present day – not merely the presentation of dry academic renderings of obscure tablets: *Sumerian Religion* will take you on a progressive journey that is just as relevant and critical today as it was thousands of years ago – *if not more so.*

Sumerian Religion is the perfect practical companion to *all systems and traditions* as it displays the origins of human traditions on the planet, something which all can relate to. As unique as it is practical – supporting a revival tradition revealing the nature, origins and traditions connected to the "Star-Gates" of the *Anunnaki Alien Gods of Mesopotamia*, which the public contemp-orary society has previously only known through nearly insubstantial renderings. A clearly understood volume offering a revolutionary perspective towards understand-ing Life, the Universe & Everything!

MARDUKITE

ABOUT THE AUTHOR:
JOSHUA FREE

First known as "Merlyn Stone" in the 1990's, **Joshua Free** reappeared on the scene in 2008 with the launch of *Mardukite Ministries* on the Summer Solstice that year.

He is now *Archbishop-Patesi* of the *Mardukite Archdiocese of North America* and the *Mardukite Chamberlains, Nabu Maerdechai*.

His prolific writings include: *Arcanum*, *Book of Elven-Faerie*, *Sumerian Religion*, *Babylonian Myth & Magic*, *Necronomicon Anunnaki Bible*, and *The Sorcerer's Handbook of Merlyn Stone* among several others.

In 2011, he released his first novel of published fiction titled *The Hybrids*.

Made in the USA
San Bernardino, CA
21 August 2014